Guns Over the Champlain Valley

Guns Over the Champlain Valley

A Guide to Historic Military Sites and Battlefields

Howard Coffin,
Will Curtis, and Jane Curtis

THE COUNTRYMAN PRESS
WOODSTOCK, VERMONT

Library of Congress Cataloging-in-Publication Data:
Coffin, Howard, 1942–
    Guns over the Champlain Valley : a guide to historic military sites and battle-
fields / Howard Coffin, Will Curtis, and Jane Curtis.—1st ed.
        p. cm.
    Includes bibliographical references and index.
    ISBN 0-88150-643-5 (alk. paper)
        1. Historic sites—Champlain Valley—Guidebooks. 2. Historic sites—New
York (State)—Guidebooks. 3. Historic sites—Vermont—Guidebooks. 4. Battle-
fields—Champlain Valley—Guidebooks. 5. Battlefields—New York (State)—
Guidebooks. 6. Battlefields—Vermont—Guidebooks. 7. Champlain
Valley—History, Military. 8. New York (State)—History, Military. 9. Vermont—
History, Military. I. Curtis, Will, 1917- II. Curtis, Jane, 1918- III. Title.

F127.C6C64 2005
974.7'54—dc22   2005045433

Excerpt on p. 90 courtesy of David Starbuck, *Rangers and Redcoats on the
Hudson: Exploring the Past on Rogers Island*, pp. 18–19. © 2004 University Press
of New England, Hanover, NH.

Cover design by Bodenweber Design
Text design and composition by Faith Hague Book Design
Maps by Jacques Chazaud
Cover photograph of Fort Ticonderoga © Thomas T. Garbelotti
Interior photographs by Howard Coffin unless otherwise specified

Published by The Countryman Press, P.O. Box 748, Woodstock,
Vermont 05091

Distributed by W.W. Norton & Company, Inc., 500 Fifth Avenue,
New York, NY 10110

Printed in the United States of America

10 9 8 7 6 5 4 3 2 1

To Peter Jennison (1922–2004),
editor, writer, founder of The Countryman Press,
and our dear, close friend.

Books by Howard Coffin

The Battered Stars: One State's Civil War Ordeal During Grant's Overland Campaign: From the Home Front in Vermont to the Battlefields of Virginia

Nine Months to Gettysburg: Stannard's Vermonters and the Repulse of Pickett's Charge

Full Duty: Vermonters in the Civil War

An Inland See: A Brief History of the Roman Catholic Diocese of Burlington

An Independent Man (with James Jeffords)

Books by Will Curtis

The Nature of Things: How and Why Things Work in the Natural World

Books by Jane Curtis and Will Curtis

Return to These Hills: The Vermont Years of Calvin Coolidge

Monhegan: The Artists' Island

The World of George Perkins Marsh
(with Frank Lieberman)

Frederick Billings: Vermonter, Pioneer Lawyer, Business Man, Conservationist: An Illustrated Biography

Contents

Foreword

ON APRIL 9, 2004, I was on another four-day speaking trip to Vermont. Since 2000, this has been an annual occurrence, and I spent a night at the home of longtime friend and colleague Howard Coffin. Howard told me that he was coauthoring, with Will and Jane Curtis, a comprehensive guidebook featuring sites associated with the military history of the Lake Champlain gateway linking the United States and Canada. He asked me if I would review the text and prepare the foreword for his and the Curtises' endeavor. Having authored forewords for three of Coffin's previous books—*Full Duty: Vermonters in the Civil War* (1993), *Nine Months to Gettysburg: Stannard's Vermonters and the Repulse of Pickett's Charge* (1997), and *The Battered Stars* (2002)—all critically acclaimed, I said yes.

The subject, because I have long admired Coffin's research and writing skills and had heard good reports about the Curtises' sleuthing skills, fired my interest. Since 1990 I have led a number of tours to the Lake Champlain and Hudson River corridors, featuring cultural sites associated with its military history, for the Smithsonian Institution travel programs and History America. Before retiring as the National Park Service's chief historian, I traveled to Vermont and upstate New York at the request of members of Congress interested in the region's historic sites, their protection, interpretation, and potential for enhanced tourism. I first met Vermont's junior senator, James Jeffords, on a memorable visit to Mount Independence in the early 1990s. About the same time, an exciting and memorable day was spent with Representative Sherwood L. Boehlert of New York's then 25th Congressional District, and key staffers. We visited cultural sites associated with the Mohawk River corridor. The day began near Rome, New York, with a stop at the Oneida Nation Territory in central New York, continued on to Fort Stanwix, the Battle of Oriskany, the Nicholas Herkimer House, and ended at Forts Klock Plain, and Canajoharie. We also met with citizen groups, as well as park managers, and preservationists.

On November 20, 1992, the day of the Windsor Castle fire in Britain, I represented the Washington, D.C. office of the National Park Service at a conference held in Glens Falls's Queensbury Hotel. It was called to rally support and discuss measures looking toward forging a public-private partnership for enhanced interpretation and preservation of the Lake Champlain corridor's national and local cultural and natural resources. It was well attended by many pro-preservationist groups. Included were Howard Coffin, representing Senator Jeffords, and senior members of the respective New York and Vermont state historic preservation offices, as well as the general public. Also present were representatives of groups like the Adirondack Solidarity Alliance, warning of what they saw as an infringement on property rights by big government. One of these people, in the question-and-answer session following my presentation, said that the Park Service, of which I was a spokesperson, harbored an agenda similar to that of Stalinist U.S.S.R. and Germany under Hitler and the Nazis. His remarks proved beneficial, because among those in attendance were Tom Mandeville and Dennis Lewis, faculty members at Clinton Community College (CCC) in Plattsburgh. They introduced themselves, and before my return to Washington, I learned of a shared interest in heritage tourism and the North Country's historic sites. They told me their dreams of employing CCC and its facilities to host annual workshops for local teachers and other interested people to introduce them to cultural sites in the Lake Champlain corridor.

I next heard from Mandeville in spring 1993, and he told me that CCC, assisted by a grant, had made their dreams a reality. He and

Lewis had developed a curriculum for week-long summer teacher-enrichment workshops titled "Historic Sites in the Champlain Corridor." Tom invited me to participate as a resource person familiar with National Park Service sites and federal historic preservation policy. This was an invitation that anyone with my interests would lust for.

Beginning in 1993 and continuing through 1996, I was privileged to spend a week annually at CCC to support this innovative program, managed by Mandeville and Lewis. After Lewis's tragic death in 1997, John Mockry, also a talented CCC faculty member, joined Mandeville as workshop cochairmen. I employ the word "innovative" in describing the program because of the cochairmen's use of visits to cultural sites that enabled participants to walk in the steps of history. It blends an appreciation of the region's unsurpassed cultural and environmental heritage and underscores that they are as relevant today as 400 years ago. The sites visited in the CCC program extended from Fort Chambly in Canada to Saratoga in the south. Accordingly, I welcomed the opportunity to prepare the foreword for *Guns Over the Champlain Valley: A Guide to Historic Military Sites and Battlefields*. I was not disappointed.

Beginning with the introductory essay that sets "the stage," and provides a context to enable the reader to better appreciate the military and political history and related sites possessing international as well as national aspirations, the book is a traveler's dream. The meat of *Guns Over the Champlain Valley* is the site locations: how to get there, along with description on facilities, fees, and amenities, that is informative and easy to understand. Sites inventoried and described are what the experienced heritage tourist would expect to find. But, better yet, the traveler is directed to several gems, such as Rokeby, Point au Fer, and other important sites, which I certainly plan to include on future regional tours.

Along with the introductory essay, the extensive narratives describing the sites and what happened there are outstanding. Significance is important in commanding space devoted to each site/museum, few are ignored. The style is graceful and commands the reader's interest.

In commending this book to the reader, I have only one regret: It was not available in 1990 when I was professionally introduced to the cultural and natural resources of the North Country and the military history of the Champlain Valley. If it had been, it would have simplified my task and shortened my learning curve.

Edwin Bearss
Chief Historian Emeritus
National Park Service

Preface

SO YOU'RE READING, or glancing at, *Guns Over the Champlain Valley*. Then you must have at least a mild interest in military history. If so, the Champlain Corridor is the place for you. The authors of this book guide you along Lake Champlain and Lake George, and the upper Hudson and Richelieu rivers; these waterways and scenic valleys constitute one of the world's most important historic landscapes. Here the decisive battles of the American Revolution and the War of 1812 took place, as did the bloodiest battle in North America before the Civil War. Here John Stark surrounded and annihilated a British force, here the northernmost land action of the Civil War happened, and here the decisive campaign of the French and Indian War transpired. Along this corridor of history stand a lakeside tavern that once sheltered Thomas Jefferson and James Madison, a house in which George Washington and Benjamin Franklin took supper, and the high walls and stone barracks of the largest fort the British ever built in North America. The bedroom where Ulysses Grant died, in a mountaintop cottage, is well preserved, as is the Adirondack farmhouse where John Brown contemplated the raid on Harpers Ferry that would ignite the mighty Civil War that Grant won. Along a wooded Vermont hillside stand fortifications built by American soldiers in 1776 and 1777, and on the once-bloodied high ground of the Saratoga Battlefield one may still walk roads used by British and American soldiers moving into battle.

In researching this book, the writers have made the wrong turns, taken the wrong roads, on the way to producing a guidebook that, we hope, is easily followed. Along the way we found that many of the important sites are hard to find. But the excitement of discovery that we experienced—the thrill of first encountering the stone ramparts of Fort Chambly, of crossing the moat into Fort Lennox, of walking the battle-grounds of Bennington and Hubbardton, still awaits the reader. With the help of this book, you can make your way to the little bay on Lake Champlain where, under fire, Benedict Arnold landed the remnants of his battered fleet after its brave fight at Valcour Island. Follow the country roads along which a bold band of Confederate bank robbers, hotly pursued by a Yankee posse, made their escape to Canada. North of Plattsburgh, find the low ridge where a few score American militia opened fire on 4,000 red-coated British veterans of the Napoleonic Wars. Atop Mount Defiance, stand where early morning light revealed the presence of British artillery, causing American troops to abandon storied Fort Ticonderoga 800 feet below. And you can explore the bluff overlooking Lake George where hundreds of terrified captives began their walk into what was the most famous massacre in American history before George Custer reached the Little Big Horn.

The authors of this book, Howard Coffin, Will Curtis, and Jane Curtis, had the same idea about the project at somewhat different times. More than a decade ago, Jane and Will, through their travels and extensive readings, had become fascinated with historic sites along Lake Champlain, particularly with the Revolutionary War campaign of British Gen. John Burgoyne. Having learned of Howard's interest in the same subject, Jane phoned him one day in 1994 and asked whether he might be interested in coauthoring a book. He replied that in order to do it right, the entire upper Hudson River, Lake George, Lake Champlain, and upper Richelieu River should be included. They readily agreed and determined that the scope of any book should range from before Samuel de Champlain's discovery of the big lake in 1609, to the Confederate raid on St. Albans in 1864. Howard told the Curtises that he had recently completed an inventory of military sites along the Champlain Corridor for Vermont's U.S. Sen. James Jeffords. All three shared, with Jeffords, a concern that the military history of the area had been somewhat forgotten and was underappreciated. All three also had learned that locating many sites and finding information about them could be difficult. Also, even the routes of military campaigns that shaped world history were not well marked for the traveler. Unlike Civil War campaigns, for which countless guidebooks exist and maps are readily available, the military history of the corridor and information on how to find the important sites could not be gleaned from any single book, or even from a small collection of titles. So the project was set about, and considerable progress was made. But soon the writing of other books got in the way, and the project languished.

Finally, in 2004, work was resumed and forays along the corridor revealed that a considerable effort had been made at many key sites to enhance interpretation. A museum had been opened at Mount Independence and new trails had been constructed. Plattsburgh has opened a center that interprets its important battles. A visitors center is now operating at Rogers Island. Rokeby is planning to open a facility that will interpret the Underground Railroad. Still, while several fine new books on corridor history had come out, including David Starbuck's *The Great Warpath* (1999), no guide for the history seeker had yet appeared.

This book is intended to introduce the reader to the stories, and help the traveler locate the sites, of the momentous conflicts that took place in this region. Those following the authors' directions will find themselves at times moving back and forth both through time and geography, discovering campaigns that had taken place where previous campaigns had been waged, some events having occurred on the same stage, yet years apart. Mind well the directions, for the roads of the corridor can be confusing, following old tracks, skirting rivers and mountains, ducking in and out of lake coves, crossing an international boundary, sometimes bearing urban traffic. Early on, the authors decided to structure the book for travelers moving south to north, for far more people live south of the corridor than to the north. This was done despite the fact that, in the key Burgoyne Campaign at least, the reader goes against time, against the campaign's day-to-day progression, in moving north along the Hudson and Lake Champlain. But with a little patience, this book is useable as a guide even for those coming from the north.

This book is written for the motorist, though, of course, there are other ways to travel the Champlain Corridor. Bike paths and bike routes abound and most major sites have information available on biking. The corridor's length can be traveled by boat using the Champlain and Chambly canals, and seeing historic sites from the water offers interesting perspectives. Also, much history is preserved beneath the waters and the Lake Champlain Maritime Museum has a wealth of information on sunken ships that divers may explore.

The authors hope that by following their recommended pathways and reading their descriptions of what happened at the individual sites, something of the wonder of the corridor's history will emerge. Time and again the authors have learned that no historic place can be well understood without a personal visit. However, this book is not meant to be a complete guide to the region's military sites. Not all historic markers and minor locations are included. And the writers seek information on additional sites and historic events for future editions. The reader is strongly urged, before setting off, to take time to read the brief history that begins this book. However, this book is written with the casual reader in mind, and therefore much information is repeated as the various sites are described. For further reading, our list of sources is a good place to start.

Guns Over the Champlain Valley is a book by three writers, long fascinated by history, who wish to share what they have found after realizing that so much important military history exists almost in their own backyards. All three writers journeying from their Vermont homes have explored the grand settings of Civil War conflicts and other distant battlefields. But we have learned that battlefields and campaigns that rival in fascination, and importance, those where the armies of Grant and Lee did battle, may be found right here near our homes.

The writers have two firm hopes. First, that the reader will find as much enjoyment as have they. Second, that in coming years, particularly with the 400th anniversary of Lake Champlain's discovery drawing near, something more will be done to unite the historic sites and make them easier to locate and appreciate. Senator Jeffords's concept of a Heritage Corridor, linking all sites with common signs and brochures, is an excellent one and should, at long last, be brought to fruition. For now, join us in traveling this beautiful land of four distinct seasons, of long lakes and prodigious mountains, of winding rivers and splashing streams, of high fields and stately forests, seeking out the sites where mighty deeds once shaped the history of the continent, the hemisphere, and the world.

Acknowledgments

THE AUTHORS OWE THANKS to many people who helped in the creation of this book. First and foremost is Edwin Cole Bearss, historian emeritus of the National Park Service, and renowned expert on military campaigns and battlefields throughout the world. Mr. Bearss has now written introductions to four Howard Coffin books, and somehow fit into his busy schedule of tour guiding and lectures not only the writing of a foreword, but a thorough reading and editing of the manuscript. Nicholas Westbrook, director of Fort Ticonderoga, generously gave of his time escorting us about the old fort and its grounds. He also patiently reviewed the page proofs, significantly improving the manuscript. Longtime friend David Starbuck, the noted archaeologist who has conducted digs at many key military sites, read the text and offered valuable suggestions. Thomas Nesbitt, historian at Crown Point, guided us around his site and those at Lake George. Many years ago, before his tragic death, Dennis Lewis helped us understand much about the history of the Plattsburgh area and we remember him fondly, and thank him. More recently Keith Herkalo, Plattsburgh city clerk, showed us his city and told us much about its history. Elsa Gilbertson and John Dumville of the Vermont Division for Historic Preservation updated us on Chimney Point and Mount Independence, while Carl Fuller, who works at the Hubbarton Battlefield, shared his extensive knowledge of the site. In Bennington, Tordis Isselhardt accompanied us on a tour of the town and the Bennington Battlefield. A lecture given in Bennington by Philip L. Lord, author of the remarkable *War over Walloomscoick*, was most helpful in our understanding of the battle. Carol B. Greenough, on two occasions, shared her immense knowledge of Whitehall and showed us the Skenesborough Museum she was instrumental in founding. JoAnne Fuller helped us understand Fort Edward and Rogers Island. At the Old Fort House Museum in Fort Edward, Cameron Spaulding was as helpful as he was enthusiastic. Don Miner and Warren Hamm shared their knowledge at the St. Albans Historical Society. Joyce Huff took time to help us understand the Ethan Allen Homestead. At Fort Lennox in Québec, Annick Guerin gave us a tour of Île-aux-Noix where the fort stands. Christine Paquette guided us around the old fort site at St. Jean. Michael Madden led us on a rare tour of Fort Montgomery, recalling a day years ago when the late Victor Podd showed us the fort that he owned, and loved. Don Craig explained the Kent-DeLord House's history. At the John Brown Farm, Brendan Mills and Linda Roy shared their extensive knowledge of the place and the complex man who once lived there. Robert Allen, author of *Marching On!*, a fine book on Brown, kindly accompanied us on a trip to the farm and shared his store of knowledge. Park Ranger Joe Craig explained the Saratoga Battlefield. Mike Barbieri welcomed us aboard the *Philadelphia II* at the Lake Champlain Maritime Museum as if he had been a member of the original boat's crew. The staffs of the Vermont Historical Society's library and the University of Vermont's Special Collections were ever helpful. Sue Limoge was supportive and helpful throughout the project, as was Howard Coffin's longtime friend from his army and newspaper days, Frank Dougherty of Philadelphia.

Chapter One

A Brief Military History of the Corridor

TO BORROW SOME WORDS from Henry Wadsworth Longfellow, the great corridor of the upper Hudson and Richelieu rivers, Lake Champlain and Lake George, was once "forest primeval." This storied land, long the domain of Native Americans, was fought over for centuries by the empire-building great powers of the earth. James Fenimore Cooper said in his *Last of the Mohicans*, a novel of the French and Indian War, that these "woods were still . . . apparently as much untenanted as when they came fresh from the hands of their Almighty Creator. The eye could range in every direction through the long and shadowed vistas of the trees; but nowhere was any object to be seen that did not properly belong to the peaceful and slumbering scenery . . . along that verdant and undulating surface of forest which spread itself unbroken, unless by stream or lake, over such a vast region of country." Historian Ralph Nading Hill called Lake Champlain "the most historic body of water in North America."

Here the nations of Europe wrested power from the Indians—the Mohawks, Iroquois, Algonquin, and Abenaki—who had existed in harmony with nature for millennia. Here the mightiest of nations waged world war for a continent, and here a new nation won its independence (a nation that was to become the most powerful in all history).

19

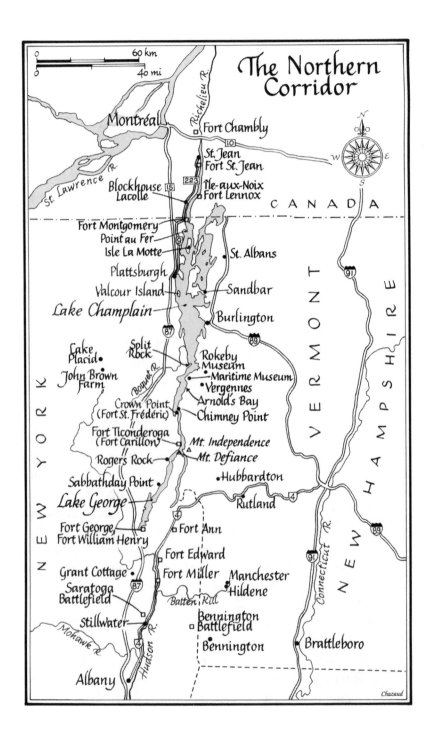

The Northern Corridor

Montréal

Fort Chambly
St. Jean
Fort St. Jean
Blockhouse
Lacolle
Île-aux-Noix
Fort Lennox

Richelieu R.
10
223
15

St. Lawrence R.

CANADA

Fort Montgomery
Point au Fer
Isle La Motte
Plattsburgh
Valcour Island
Lake Champlain
9

St. Albans
Sandbar
Burlington

87
89

Lake Placid
John Brown Farm
Split Rock
Crown Point (Fort St. Frédéric)
Fort Ticonderoga (Fort Carillon)
Rogers Rock
Sabbathday Point
Lake George
Fort George
Fort William Henry
Grant Cottage
Saratoga Battlefield
Stillwater
Albany

Boquet R.

Rokeby Museum
Maritime Museum
Vergennes
Arnold's Bay
Chimney Point
Mt. Independence
Mt. Defiance
Hubbardton
Rutland

VERMONT

91

NEW HAMPSHIRE

4
89

Fort Ann
Fort Edward
Fort Miller
Manchester
Hildene
Bennington Battlefield
Bennington

Batten Kill

Mohawk R.
Hudson R.
87
4

Connecticut R.
91

NEW HAMPSHIRE

Brattleboro

NEW YORK

0   60 km
0   40 mi

N
W   E
S

Chazaud

To these uncharted wilds came Europeans, strangers in a strange land, among them the explorer Samuel de Champlain and the Black Robes with their doomed Father Isaac Jogues. To these hills and valleys came the Marquis de Montcalm, the brave George-Augustus Viscount Howe, George Washington, Thomas Jefferson, Benjamin Franklin, Philip Schuyler, and Ethan Allen. These fabled lakes and rivers knew Benedict Arnold, then in his glory fighting for America, the brilliant Tadeusz Kosciuszko, bold Seth Warner, fiery John Stark, Sir Guy Carleton, and "Gentleman" John Burgoyne. And here walked Robert Rogers and his Rangers, Baron Friedrich Adolph von Riedesel, Arthur St. Clair, Paul Revere, Anthony Wayne, the terrified captives seized at Fort William Henry, and Duncan Campbell, haunted by words of a spectre foretelling his death at a place called Ticonderoga.

Along these valleys came escaped slaves, spirited toward freedom in Canada by other freedom-loving people. And here came Confederate raiders to fight the northernmost land action of the Civil War. Here the scalp of Jane McCrea was lifted, causing farmers to abandon plows and take up arms to fight an army of the British Empire. Here Commodore Thomas Macdonough traded broadsides with a British fleet off Plattsburgh, as the decks ran red with blood.

For nearly 250 years after the coming of Europeans, the valleys of the upper Hudson River, Lake George, Lake Champlain, and the Richelieu River were touched by fire. And, fortunately, the people of this 120-mile-long corridor have had the good sense to preserve many of the places associated with these long-ago conflicts. Because this area's history ties into the history of far-flung areas, west along the Mohawk River and beyond, south to New York City, north to walled Québec City, along Arnold's route of invasion to the Maine coast, even to Louisburg in Nova Scotia, limits had to be set. The northern boundary of our corridor is the old stone fortress at Chambly, on the great river bend where long rapids suddenly make the Richelieu unnavigable. Built in the reign of Louis XV, this brooding old bastion is of a time when kings reigned and power was held by a privileged few. In the summer of 1777, Gentleman John Burgoyne and his powerful army of empire moved south from Chambly, bound to batter a new nation born of rebellion into defeat. We mark the southern extremity of our corridor on the high fields of Saratoga, where the Neilson House that witnessed the Revolutionary War's decisive battle still stands. Within sight of the house, as high autumn and the blood of British soldiers reddened the fallen Hudson Valley leaves of 1777, a crushing de-

---

The Rapids Remember

At Fort Chambly, beside the rushing Richelieu River, an interpretive sign tells us that THE RAPIDS REMEMBER. And so do the lakes and hills, forests and mountains, ramparts and redoubts. The people who played out the events that created this monumental story left us their words. Hear Jabez Fitch, Jr., one of Rogers' Rangers, stationed far from home on the frontier at Fort Edward in the winter of 1758:

> ye Snows Have Fell Repeatedly one after another. We Have Constantly Kept a Good Slay Path out in the One Plais and if a Man Steps out of this Path (Unless he Has on Snow Shoes) ye Snow will Take Him in Past ye Middle–This Morning, after ye Covering Party Had Gon out, & a Great Number of Men (with out Arms) with their Slays for Wood Both of ye Ragulars & Connecticutts the Enimy Attacted them . . . ye Indians (Being Provided with Snow Shoes So as to Go any Where) heded them, & (in our Sight Drove them Back into ye Woods Like So many Sheep or Cattle) where they Tomahawkd Kild & Scalpd them, or Carryd them away Prisoners . . . In this Days Action, there was a Serjt & 11 Men of ye Ragulars Kild & Scalpd 4 Wounded & 6 Mising–& one of Capt Putnam's Men Kild, which is Jedediah Lee–& No other Man Hurt Except ye Ragulars–Among Others Serjt Cooper Shared In this Sad Fate and Maj Renols our Old Neighbour, Who Has Made Us So Much Laugh & Sport, Has Fell a Victim to those Savages–This Morning when I Awoak I thought My Self Obligd to Observe My Dreems, as they Run Vastly upon Green Flowery Gardens and Every thing Seemd to Appear Gay as in ye Month of May. Dreems of this Kind I Never Knew Fale, But What Something Dreadfull Followd . . .

feat was inflicted on Burgoyne's army that guaranteed a new nation's independence. The quiet dignity of the Neilsons' frontier cabin is thoroughly American, the home of people living in the freedom they helped to win, suddenly having a say in their nation's destiny, suddenly with a chance to rise as far as their abilities, and hard work, would take them. We mark the southern limit of our corridor at the Neilson House, on the high fields of the Saratoga National Battlefield Park.

A BRIEF PREHISTORY

Before summarizing the military history of this once great wilderness, we should touch upon the region's prehistory, about which we know relatively little, except from legends and evidence unearthed by archaeologists and geologists. Mighty forces of nature shaped the landscape within which great human dramas would unfold. Today, driving up the busy Northway skirting New York's towering Adirondacks, or along Vermont's Route 22A past summer fields with the long ridge of the Green Mountains beyond, it is hard to imagine a time 20,000 years ago when a mile-high glacier covered much of North America: grinding its way south, shaving the tops of mountains, gouging the Hudson-Champlain Trench, rearranging the landscape, its weight pressed down the earth.

The glacial bulldozer ground to a halt when it reached Long Island and Nantucket 15,000 years ago. Then it began a long, messy, wet retreat for more thousands of years, leaving a scoured, gravelly landscape interspersed with frigid glacial lakes whose ancient beaches can still be seen. The land had not recovered from the ice's oppressive weight when the ocean rolled up the St. Lawrence River and into the Champlain Valley around 12,800 years ago, creating the vast inland Champlain Sea in which coral reefs were laid down, seals basked, and whales spouted. Finally, the land rose and the sea drained, leaving a freshwater lake whose current still flows down the Richelieu River to the St. Lawrence. Lake George, 200 feet higher and isolated in its narrow valley, also flows north into far larger Champlain.

New rivers cut through gravel debris, creating a watery passageway and connecting the mid-Atlantic Ocean with the St. Lawrence River. In the museum at Whitehall, New York, we learn that it was possible to journey from Chambly on the Richelieu to New York City by crossing only 20 miles of dry land. This water highway, with connections to the Great Lakes and Mohawk Valley via the St. Lawrence, was the chief pathway of the region for thousands of years.

Paleobotanists find that the landscape then resembled vast parks of grasslands interspersed with clumps of spruce, alder, and poplar. Mastodons and woolly mammoths moved north with the plants, as did moose, elk, giant beaver, and caribou. Finally, about 10,500 B.C., roving bands of Paleo-Indians, following game along the river valleys, came to live in this corridor near its streams and lakes, where their stone tools and their ceramics have been found, fashioned toward the end of the prehistoric era. The succession of styles—from 12,000-year-old fluted spear points to arrowheads made in A.D. 300—establish a time line over thousands of years of slow, cautious change.

Small bands of perhaps 50 people each lived a subsistence existence foraging for plants, hunting porcupines, rabbits, and even large animals. Their clothes and houses were of skin. Weapons were spears, or lances used at close quarters. Tools included knives, scrapers, awls, hammer stones, and drills, rudimentary but made of such high-quality stone as chert (a flintlike rock). Some fine stone reached the local toolmakers from hundreds of miles away, either through trading or perhaps gathered while following the inexhaustible caribou. Fluted spear points made by Paleo-Indians have been found at many sites, including throughout the Champlain lowlands, along the Missisquoi River, in the upper Winooski River's watershed, at Crown Point, and near the northern end of the portage connecting the Hudson River and Lake George.

The Paleo-Indian culture, which lasted more than 2,000 years, was succeeded by the Archaic period, the Early Archaic, Middle Archaic, and Late Archaic periods—altogether, they lasted 8,000 years, to about 1000 B.C. Simultaneously, the landscape changed from open grasslands to forests, as pine, oak, hemlock, and beech spread north. For a wider variety of game, a more sophisticated level of weaponry had to develop. People settled into a territorial life, living in dome-shaped houses of saplings covered with bark strips. Their tool kits included awls, axes, chisels, and gouges for making dugout canoes. Early Archaic period artifacts, of local stone, have been widely discovered, at Swanton and near Lake George, for instance.

Middle Archaic period sites have been found near Ferrisburgh, on Otter Creek, near Lake Bomoseen, and on the Batten Kill River. Late Archaic sites lie along Otter Creek, near the mouth of Little Ausable River, and in the Glens Falls area. Their inhabitants possessed a broad array of woodworking, fishing, and hunting tools distinct from those of their ancestors, and they had apparently learned to make birch-bark canoes. As this late period ended, elaborate burials became fashionable, and from cemeteries found on Isle La Motte and East Creek come copper beads, shell, and walrus-tooth gorgets (ornamental collars) indicating a far-flung trading system.

Languages had been evolving through the long years and most inhabitants of eastern North America spoke some variant of Algonquian. But smaller groups living near the Great Lakes and along the Mohawk were Iroquoian-speakers.

About A.D. 1000, the Hudson-Champlain region warmed, making agriculture possible farther north and bringing more people. In one such movement, Iroquoian speakers moved from the Great Lakes into the upper St. Lawrence Valley. The Iroquoian people, including the Oneida, Onondaga, Cayuga, and Seneca peoples, lived to the west of the Mohawk River. The Mohawks lived along the river in fortified villages. By moving into the St. Lawrence Valley, the Laurentian Iroquois isolated the Abenaki people of the Champlain and evicted them from the western side of the big lake. Hence, tensions were increasing, particularly with the forming of the powerful Five Nation Confederation around A.D. 1400. The Champlain Valley seems to have become a no-man's-land, a buffer zone, through which people traveled, but did not settle.

TRIBAL CONFLICT AND THE EUROPEANS

Tribal conflict became inevitable with the fur trade, and even before Europeans ventured into the interior their steel knives, iron pots, axes, cloth, and guns were reaching the native peoples through trade. In the mid-1600s the Dutch, later supplanted by the English, established trading posts along the Hudson River, while the French did the same on the Richelieu River and lower Lake Champlain. Territories that had been hunting grounds now became trapping grounds for beaver pelts that were highly valued in Europe—they became lands to fight over. The Mohicans, defeated by the Mohawks as suppliers of fur to the Europeans, disappeared from the region. After the traders came the settlers, and the ensuing clash of cultures forever changed the Indians' world. It was inevitable, too, that the Indians became involved in the so-called White Man's wars, became pawns in the Europeans' struggle for control of North America.

In 1609, recorded history came to the region with the arrival of the French explorer Champlain. "Had it not been for the compulsion of Samuel de Champlain to write down what he saw and heard," wrote historian Ralph Nading Hill, "the beginning of the recorded history of Lake Champlain might have been indefinitely postponed. Although Columbus had long preceded him, little knowledge about the interior of North America had accumulated. When Champlain's canoe emerged from the Richelieu onto the shining lake in July 1609, the only European settlements on the continent other than Port Royal and his own at Quebec were those of the Spaniards in Florida and Mexico and Britain's two-year-old colony at Jamestown."

Champlain was in the company of Algonquins as he ventured against the current of the Richelieu River and entered the great body of water that later would bear his name. Asking an Indian guide whether the new lands were peopled, he related that "they told me that they were—by the Iroquois—and that in these places there were beautiful valleys and other stretches fertile in grain such as I had eaten in this country, with a great many other fruits."

Somewhere well up the lake on a prominent point of land, probably either at Ticonderoga or Crown Point, Champlain and his party encountered Iroquois warriors. After a night of exchanging insults, a battle commenced that ended when Champlain and his fellow French, armed with the primitive musket they called "arquebus," slew several Iroquois, among them two chiefs. "When I saw them making a move to shoot us," Champlain wrote, "I rested my arquebus against my cheek and aimed directly at one of the three chiefs. With the same shot two of them fell to the ground, and one of their companions, who was wounded and afterwards died."

The French founded Montréal in 1642 and then began building forts to the south, on the Richelieu at Chambly and Sainte-Therese, and then, in 1666, Fort St. Anne was erected on the northern tip of Isle La Motte. The wooden stockade surrounding several buildings was abandoned in 1671. By that time the first of the Black Robes—French Catholic missionaries who were hated by the Indians—had ventured into the wilds hoping to convert the native population. Among them was Father Isaac Jogues, a Jesuit, who was captured by Indians and

---

From *The Last of the Mohicans*

James Fenimore Cooper, beginning his novel, which is set during the French and Indian War, wrote:

> It was a feature peculiar to the colonial wars of North America, that the toils and dangers of the wilderness were to be encountered before the adverse hosts could meet. A wide and apparently an impervious boundary of forests severed the possessions of the hostile provinces of France and England. The hardy colonist, and the trained European who fought at his side, frequently expended months in struggling against the rapids of the streams, or in effecting the rugged passes of the mountains, in quest of an opportunity to exhibit their courage in a more martial conflict. But, emulating the patience and self-denial of the practiced native warriors, they learned to overcome every difficulty; and it would seem that, in time, there were no recess of the woods so dark nor any secret place so lovely, that it might claim exemption from the inroads of those who had pledged their blood to satiate their vengeance, or to uphold the cold and selfish policy of the distant monarchs of Europe.

taken up the Richelieu and through Lake Champlain and Lake George, christening the latter Lac du St. Sacrement. Perhaps on what is now called Jogues Island, near Westport, the priest was forced to run the gauntlet. He was tortured time and again; finally, one of his female Indian converts was forced to chew his fingers until they were horribly deformed. Freed at long last, the priest briefly returned to France. Pleading with superiors to return him to the wilds, Father Jogues was back in the New World in 1646 where he was again captured and this time executed with a tomahawk.

The next fort on the lake was built by Jacobus de Warm, a Dutchman perhaps working for the English, at Chimney Point in 1690. The tiny fortification rose by a lake now claimed by both France and England and becoming ever more highly prized in the now-beginning French and Indian War, conflicts that would last three-quarters of a century.

Raiding parties now moved up and down the corridor burning villages as far north as Montréal, west along the Mohawk Valley, and south and east to Deerfield, Massachusetts, on the Connecticut River, and Albany on the Hudson. The Deerfield Raid, on a chill winter night in 1704, was particularly bloody. The Rev. John Williams, seized by the French and Indians, looked back at his parish from a hilltop and "saw the smoke of the fires in town and beheld the awful desolation of Deerfield, and before we marched any farther they killed a suckling child of the English." Williams and other survivors were taken through the snow-clad hills of Vermont to the Winooski Valley, and then down Champlain to Canada. Many captives were killed, including Williams's wife, weak from recent childbirth and unable to keep pace. The captors, Williams said, "Made me take a last farewell of my dear wife, the desire of my eyes and companion in many mercies and afflictions." One stroke of a tomahawk killed her. Raids continued until 1780, when English and Indians attacked the village of Royalton on Vermont's White River.

In 1731, the French enlarged the old British fort at Chimney Point and a settlement of some 300 inhabitants grew around it. On the opposite shore, less than a quarter mile across the narrows, the French built a much more substantial stone fortress at Crown Point.

Stone fortress at Crown Point

Fort St. Frederic lorded over the lake like a castle, with a keep four-stories high, a drawbridge, 20 cannon, and walls 20 feet thick. Several hundred yards to the south, on the shore, stood a stone windmill also equipped with cannon that served as a lookout to the south, toward the English. Another small settlement quickly developed nearby.

THE GREAT CONFLICTS BEGIN

As the French fortified their southern frontier, so the English strengthened their northern frontier. In 1755 they built Fort Edward at the Great Carrying Place on the Hudson River, where rapids make the river unnavigable. That year a French force under Baron Dieskau moved to attack the new fort, but realized they lacked enough men for an assault. Intercepted by the British just south of the southern tip of Lake George, the Battle of Lake George began. The British quickly threw up rough entrenchments and, in a vicious fight, withstood a French attack. Finally, the British and their Indian allies "sprang over the breastwork and followed them like lions and made terrible havoc and soon brought arms full of guns, laced hats, and cartridge boxes," according to one eyewitness. Dieskau, three times wounded, was saved only by the intervention of the British commander William Johnson.

The British then set about building a fort on the battlefield on the bluff at the southern end of Lake George. Named Fort William Henry, it was described many years later by historian Francis Parkman as "an irregular bastioned square, formed by embankments of gravel surmounted by a rampart of heavy logs, laid in tiers crossed one upon another, the interstices filled with earth. The lake protected it from the north, the marsh to the east, and ditches with *cheveaux-de-frise* (pointed stakes) on the south and west. Seventeen cannon, great and small, besides seven mortars and swivels, were mounted upon it . . . " In 1755, the French, realizing that their defenses along Champlain needed more than deteriorating Fort St. Frederic, began building another fort to the south at another lake narrows. Constructed at a place called Ticonderoga near the outflow of Lake George, they called it Carillon. Fort Carillon, now the French front line, built mainly of wood and earth with outer works and a sawmill, was later reconstructed of stone.

At the very beginning of that year, in deep winter, well before the coming of the geese, the French had tried to capture Fort William

Fort William Henry

The "Seat of War"

After a relatively quiet year of fort building in 1756, came the fateful and furious year of 1757. Francis Parkman sets the scene as winter has ended:

> Spring came at last, and the Dutch burghers of Albany heard, faint from the far height, the clamor of the wildfowl, streaming in long lines northward to their summer home. As the aerial travellers winged their way, the seat of war lay spread beneath them like a map. First the blue Hudson, Half-Moon, Stillwater, Saratoga, and the geometric lines and earthen mounds of Fort Edward. Then the broad belt of dingy evergreen; and beyond, released from wintry fetters, the glistening breast of Lake George, with Fort William Henry at its side, amid charred ruins and a desolation of prostrate forests. Hence the lake stretched northward, like some broad river, trenched between mountain ranges still leafless and gray. Then they looked down on Ticonderoga, with the flag of the Bourbons, like a flickering white speck, waving on its ramparts; and next on Crown Point with its tower of stone. Lake Champlain now spread before them, widening as they flew: on the left, the mountain wilderness of the Adirondacks, like a stormy sea congealed; on the right, the long procession of the Green Mountains; and, far beyond, on the dim verge of the eastern sky, the White Mountains throned in savage solitude. They passed over the bastioned square of Fort St. Jean, Fort Chambly guarding the rapids of the Richelieu, and the broad belt of the St. Lawrence, with Montréal seated on its bank. Here we leave them, to build their nests and hatch their brood among the fens of the lonely North.

Henry. But its small garrison saw the much larger French force's approach, was well prepared, and able to discourage an assault. Before they departed, the French burned all the fort's outbuildings, leaving William Henry, as Parkman said, "amid charred ruins and a desolation of prostrate forests."

As the warm months arrived, the Marquis de Montcalm with an 8,000-man army of French regulars, Canadian militia, and Indians, embarked at the northern end of Lake George to assault Fort William Henry. This time it was a major offensive as the largest army yet seen on the continent laid siege to the fort and its badly outnumbered garrison. Montcalm sent the commander a message that read in part, "I owe it to humanity to summon you to surrender. At present I can restrain the savages and make them observe the terms of a capitulation." Lt. Col. George Monro, a Scotsman, replied that he would defend the fort to the last man. The defenders fought valiantly as the French pushed their lines and siege guns ever closer. But cannon battered the fort's walls, and in just six days Monro surrendered. As Montcalm had warned, he was unable to control parts of his force, and many members of the British garrison were massacred. Montcalm finally went among the Indians to appeal for order, and lives were saved. The survivors made their way to Fort Edward, where a garrison of some 4,000 men waited, never ordered to the defense of Fort William Henry by the hapless commander, General Daniel Webb.

In the summer of 1758, a still larger army, this one British with 15,000 men under James Abercromby, moved down Lake George in a seemingly endless column of boats for an attack on Fort Carillon, held by Montcalm and just 3,600 men. In the advance of the British force were Robert Rogers and his Rangers; near the fort they encircled 350 French, and most were either killed or captured. But the victory proved most costly to the English, as Abercromby's second in command, George-Augustus Viscount Howe, was killed. Howe, beloved by his men and a brave soldier who often accompanied Rogers' Rangers on their dangerous forays, was once praised by Gen. James Wolfe as "the noblest Englishman that has appeared in my time, and the best soldier in the British army." Britain's hopes to win an entire continent may have died with him.

Abercromby's large force closed on Carillon, and the general ordered a frontal assault on the fort's well-prepared but undermanned outer works. British regulars fell in waves, with the Black Watch Regiment taking particularly heavy casualties. Francis Parkman wrote:

The scene was frightful: masses of infuriated men who could not go forward and would not go back; straining for an enemy they could not reach, firing on an enemy they could not see; caught in the entanglement of fallen trees; tripped by briars, stumbling over logs, tearing through boughs; shouting, yelling, cursing, and pelted all the while with bullets that killed them by scores, stretched them on the ground, or hung them on jagged branches in strange attitudes of death.

Among those shot at the French earthworks was Duncan Campbell, of the Black Watch, whose doom at a place called Ticonderoga had been foretold in the Scottish highlands many years before, according to legend, by the apparition of a murdered man.

If the defeat was a severe one for the British, French domination of the lake named for their pioneer explorer Champlain was swiftly nearing its end. Jeffery Amherst, ever cautious but also resolute, now appeared on the scene with a grand strategy. Amherst would march on Ticonderoga and Crown Point and, seizing them, advance into Canada and against Montréal. Meanwhile, General Wolfe would move up the St. Lawrence Valley, while another army of the king advanced to the west against Fort Niagara. With some 9,000 men, Amherst himself moved north from Fort Edward in the early summer of 1759, and on reaching the site of Fort William Henry, he ordered a new bastion to be built just to the east—Fort George. In mid-July, Amherst's force embarked by boat, bound north on Lake George for Ticonderoga. As the British approached, most of the outnumbered defenders quickly set sail for Crown Point, leaving but a small garrison. When Amherst closed on the ramparts, bringing up cannon, the French departed, touching off barrels of gunpowder as they left that severely damaged the fort. Amherst moved against Crown Point, arriving to find it abandoned and Fort St. Frederic blown up. The strongpoints of the French were thus falling like tenpins, and Amherst ordered another fort built at Crown Point, a huge bastion to be built to the west of the old French citadel.

His Majesty's Fort at Crown Point became the largest ever constructed by the British in North America. Indeed, the final bill to the

Crown of several million pounds raised eyebrows in London. Amherst also sent a detachment east across the lake to build a road from the shore near Chimney Point over the Green Mountains to The Fort at Number Four at Charlestown, New Hampshire. This road would be an avenue of settlement for much of what would become Vermont.

Throughout this period, the British had in Rogers' Rangers a most potent weapon that the French were never able to deter. "Their captain was Robert Rogers, of New Hampshire," wrote Parkman, "a strong, well-knit figure, in dress and appearance more woodsman than soldier, with a clear, bold eye, and features that would have been good but for the ungainly proportions of the nose. He was ambitious and violent, yet able in more ways than one, by no means uneducated, and so skilled in woodcraft, so energetic and resolute, that his services were invaluable." The Rangers scouted, raided, and ambushed French forces and their Indian allies. The wilderness between Fort Edward, where they often camped on nearby Rogers Island, and Fort Ticonderoga, whose garrison they ever threatened, was their domain. Historian Ralph Nading Hill wrote:

> In their many sorties on skates, snowshoes and in whaleboats near Ticonderoga, the Rangers generally inflicted more punishment than they received, although their losses were occasionally very heavy. During the Abercromby campaign one of the more illustrious Rangers, Israel Putnam, was sent to Fiddler's Elbow in the Champlain Narrows to intercept any French scouts or detachments trying to approach the British from that direction. Putnam had only a few men and chose as the point of ambush a high ledge known today as Put's Rock. When 500 French and Indians passed below in the moonlight Putnam opened fire, killing half the enemy while losing only one ranger.

The Rangers' most famous adventure occurred in the autumn of 1759, when Amherst ordered Rogers to move north and deal, once and for all, with the Abenakis. The Rangers set out from Crown Point on a raid against the St. Francis Indian village well up on the St. Lawrence River. In an assault at first light, Rogers claimed an overwhelming victory, though recent historians contend that the Abenakis knew of

Rogers' approach and that the attack was really a failure. Rogers wrote: "About seven o'clock in the morning the affair was completely over, in which time we had killed at least two hundred Indians and taken twenty of their women and children prisoners, fifteen of whom I let go on their own way, and five I brought with me, namely, two Indian boys and three Indian girls. I likewise took five English captives."

The Rangers' retreat—through the chill wilds of Québec to Lake Memphremagog and on through Vermont to the Connecticut River—was agonizing. Pursued by Indian and French and short of food, Rogers finally left his men in the Connecticut's Oxbow Country and rafted downriver seeking help at The Fort at Number Four. When a rescue party finally arrived, 49 men had been lost to starvation and the enemy.

Amherst's grand strategy went forward. To the west, Fort Niagara fell. Wolfe moved against Québec and captured the walled city, though both he and Montcalm died fighting on the Plains of Abraham. A British army from Crown Point in 1760 cut off a French force at Île-aux-Noix in the Richelieu. The British then combined forces to attack Montréal, which promptly surrendered. In the Treaty of Paris, signed on February 10, 1763, France gave up most of its claims to North America. Amherst was a grand hero of the empire. Historian Bruce Lancaster wrote:

> The Treaty of Paris ushered in a brief span of time upon which British North Americans would look back a few years later as a sort of Golden Age. No hostile power threatened. The whole Atlantic coastline and its shallow, thinly settled hinterland belonged to England and to the thousands of transplanted Europeans, mostly from the British Isles, who had flocked to the New World, since the dawn of the previous century. The prospect was dazzling.

But this "Golden Age" was to be short-lived for the Hudson, Lake George, Lake Champlain, and the Richelieu Corridor. Particularly in the land between Champlain and the Connecticut, territorial disputes among the settlers that often involved the Allen Brothers, at times, became bloody. To the south, in Massachusetts, discontent with British rule was building toward open revolt. The rebellion broke out in April 1775 on Lexington Green and by the "rude bridge" at nearby Concord.

REVOLUTION

Ethan Allen, a frontier philosopher and born fighter, a Connecticut native transplanted to Vermont, immediately determined to bring Fort Ticonderoga under American control. Ticonderoga, though along with Crown Point still the best-known British bastion in North America, was in a state of disrepair and garrisoned by only about 50 men. Allen and his Green Mountain Boys, joined by Benedict Arnold, crossed Lake Champlain from Hands Cove in the predawn of May 10, 1775, and easily captured the fort. It was the first American offensive action of the Revolutionary War. Allen addressed his men before the attack: "Friends and fellow soldiers—You have, for a number of years past, been a scourge and terror to arbitrary power. Your valor has been famed abroad, and acknowledged, as appears by the advice and orders to me from the general assembly of Connecticut, to surprise and take the garrison before you, and in person conduct you through the wicket gate; for we must this morning either quit our pretensions to valour or possess ourselves of this fortress in a few minutes. And in as much as it is a desperate attempt, which none but the bravest of men dare undertake, I do not urge it on any contrary to his will. You that will undertake voluntarily, poise your firelocks."

It was easier than the warning indicated, as Allen's men overcame just one drowsy sentry. Rushing to the quarters of the British officer in charge, Allen was asked in whose name surrender was demanded. "In the name of the Great Jehovah and the Continental Congress," he roared. Allen then dispatched Seth Warner to take the big fort at Crown Point, even more lightly defended. As winter came on, 59 cannon seized at the two forts were dispatched to Boston, where Washington confronted the British. "Col. Knox, of the artillery, came to camp," Gen. William Heath wrote in his journal on January 18. "He brought from Ticonderoga a fine train of artillery which had been taken from the British, both cannon and mortars." Henry Knox, a Boston bookseller before the war, had placed the guns on sleds and dragged them by horse and ox over snow-covered New York and Massachusetts mountains and valleys. Washington placed the guns on Dorchester Heights, overlooking Boston and its harbor. The British sailed away.

Allen and Arnold were full of fight; using a sloop seized at White-hall from the Tory Philip Skene, Arnold set off down the lake and into the Richelieu to capture the British garrison at St. Jean. Allen was also en route in slower boats and met the triumphant Arnold coming south with a captured British ship. "Arnold sailed with the prize and schooner for Ticonderoga," said Allen, "when I met him with my party, within a few miles of St. John's, he saluted me with a discharge of cannon, which I returned with a volley of small arms: This being repeated three times, I went on board the sloop with my party, where several loyal Congress healths were drank. We were now masters of Lake Champlain."

That small success helped prompt another American invasion of Canada, with Richard Montgomery in command, who sailed in late summer of 1775 from Crown Point. From the first the expedition was plagued by sickness, and two early attempts at capturing the British base at St. Jean failed. But the Americans moved north, cutting off any chance of reinforcements, and on October 18 they forced the surrender of the fort at Chambly. Back at St. Jean, Montgomery's forces began a heavy bombardment of the British fortifications, to which the British replied with some 2,500 shells. On November 1, after a six-hour bombardment, Montgomery demanded surrender. It came days later as the garrison of 600 marched out of the fort to lay down arms. Meanwhile, Allen set off for the St. Lawrence to attack Montréal. "I had but 45 men with me;" Allen wrote, "some of whom were wounded: the enemy kept closing round me; nor was it in my power to prevent it, by which means, my situation which was advantageous in the first part of the attack ceased to be in the last; and being almost entirely surrounded but with vast unequal numbers, I ordered a retreat, but found that the enemy, who were of the country and their Indians, could run as fast as my men." Allen was captured and shipped to England, a prisoner, quarantined from the rest of the American Revolution.

Montgomery, with a much larger force, then advanced on Montréal, succeeding where Allen had failed. Then he moved up the St. Lawrence to join Arnold, who had marched overland from Maine, in a wintertime attack on Québec. Seth Warner and John Stark were in joint command of troops sent to Canada as reinforcements. A three-person commission that included Benjamin Franklin came north from Philadelphia for a look at the war effort in Canada. Stops were made at Ticonderoga, Crown Point, Arnold's Bay, and Essex, with the 70-year-old Franklin wrapped in blankets against the chill north wind. Suffering an attack of gout, he complained that he became feebler each day.

Montgomery was killed at Québec and Arnold was wounded. The campaign was collapsing. A doctor with the army wrote: "Fortune and the country seemed jointly against us . . . Our prospect was gloomy. A committee from Congress had been in Montréal for some time . . . but it answered no purpose. General Thomas (as he had feared) caught the smallpox, sickened and died. Soon after this, General Sullivan (of New Hampshire) arrived and took the command. Arnold turned over command and, plagued by smallpox and pressed by a British force under Guy Carleton, the Americans retreated from Canada. The diseased army came to rest at Crown Point, with the smallpox-afflicted shipped across the lake to Hospital Creek, and to a hospital at the southern end of Lake George."

On July 7, 1776, three days after the Declaration of Independence was signed in Philadelphia, American forces abandoned Crown Point and withdrew to Ticonderoga, against the wishes of General Washington. The strategic importance of a rocky peninsula opposite the fort had been previously noticed by Franklin, John Trumbull, and Philip Schuyler, who wrote Washington that it was "so remarkably strong as to require little labor to make it tenable against a vast superiority of force, and fully to answer the purpose of preventing the enemy from penetrating into the country south of it." "Surrounded as it is on three sides by walls of natural rock," historian Ralph Nading Hill wrote, "and on the fourth by a creek, Schuyler was convinced that 20,000 men could not drive away a quarter that many defending it. Accordingly, the forest was cleared from its summit 200 feet above the lake, batteries erected, and three brigades were transferred from Ticonderoga. Later a hospital was erected and a star-shaped fort of pickets surrounding a square of barracks."

Pounding north from Philadelphia by horseback, over the rude roads and trails of the new nation, riders bore the new Declaration of Independence. They reached the new fort on July 18, and the *Boston*

Gazette reported: "Immediately after divine worship the Declaration of Independence was read by Colonel St. Clair, and having said, 'God save the free independent States of America!' the army manifested their joy with three cheers." The newly fortified peninsula, soon to be manned with 10,000 troops and bristling with guns, was christened Mount Independence.

Benedict Arnold, having recovered his health after the Canadian campaign, was now back in fighting form, and with Schuyler he set to work at Skenesborough, at the lake's southern tip, building an American fleet for Lake Champlain. High wages were advertised and experienced ship workers quickly arrived from major ports along the Atlantic coast. The Americans knew well that the British were fast assembling a Champlain fleet on the Richelieu at St. Jean. The new American fleet, built of green wood, save for two captured British vessels, was rowed north to Independence to receive masts. On August 24, Arnold put out from Crown Point with the fleet of nine boats. Bad weather forced him back, and it was September 23 before the little fleet with its amateur sailors anchored in the narrow channel between Valcour Island and the New York shore. Aboard his flagship, the *Royal Savage*, Arnold appealed in vain to be sent experienced sailors as he waited for the inevitable arrival of the mighty British lake fleet, carrying 700 experienced seamen. American Major James Wilkinson wrote: "He formed a line . . . in the narrow pass between . . . Valcour Island and the main and came to anchor, his flanks being secured by the opposite shores . . . Arnold had withdrawn himself behind this island, and so near to the main that he could not be discovered by the enemy until they had turned the southern point of it. Early on the morning of the 11th . . . Arnold's guard boats warned him of the approach of the enemy under a press of sail with a fresh breeze from the northwest."

The battle lasted all day, with Arnold himself often aiming cannon. The British drew off in late afternoon, having given the outgunned Americans a considerable battering, meaning to finish the job next day. That night, Arnold ordered what remained of his fleet to move south along the New York shore, all lights out, all men remaining silent. A fog rolled in toward morning and at sunrise the Americans had a good head start by the time the British discovered the escape.

A running battle ensued. Arnold was forced to abandon hope of reaching his Crown Point destination. Instead, he steered what was left of his fleet into a little bay on the lake's east shore, a place now called Arnold's Bay. There he torched his remaining ships, while the British fleet, drawn up at the bay's entrance, opened fire. The survivors scrambled up the bluffs and made their way overland to safety. Meanwhile, the British under Sir Guy Carleton, intending at once to attack Ticonderoga, ran into foul weather. It was not until October 28 that Carleton sent three ships south to feel out the American defenses. Arriving at Three Mile Point, they were confronted by an awesome sight. Before them, with flags flying, were Mount Independence and Fort Ticonderoga, with their 13,000-man garrison turned out for war. Carleton sent one ship down the narrow channel, which was quickly met with cannonballs. He took a long look, then turned north, bound for Canada in which to pass the winter. The British plan to race down Champlain and the Hudson in the summer of 1776 had been abandoned.

Fort Ticonderoga from Mount Independence horseshoe battery in Orwell, Vermont.

VERMONT DIVISION FOR HISTORIC PRESERVATION

A hard North Country winter settled in. The garrison at Ticon-deroga/Independence was promptly cut to about 3,000 men, and those left behind prepared to ride out the cold months as best they could on their windy points of rock. Smallpox and fever, which had appeared during the building of the new fortifications, persisted. The cold deepened and food was in short supply. One night, several men froze to death in their huts and tents, a few of the hundreds who are believed to have died, and been buried, on The Mount.

In the spring of 1777, Arthur St. Clair was in command at Inde-pendence and Ticonderoga and expecting the return of the British, who came by lake and by land in an expeditionary force under the command of John Burgoyne. Burgoyne, a playwright who had distin-guished himself in military campaigns in Portugal, was known as a moderate concerning the American cause. His grand strategy was to move his army of 8,000 from Canada along Champlain, while a British force came north from New York City, and still another moved east along the Mohawk Valley. When all three forces met, the isolation of New England, it was hoped, would have been accomplished.

Burgoyne first issued a proclamation to the peoples of the rebelling lands asking their cooperation and threatening "devastation, famine and other concomitant horror" to those who opposed him. Those words, of course, alarmed the populace, which always lived in fear of raids and knew that Indians accompanied the British army. Burgoyne encamped at Button Mould Bay on the Vermont shore on June 25. Hill wrote: "The spectacle of the diverse flotilla was rivaled by the bril-liant patchwork of its cargo, the Indians in war paint, the German and English regulars in white, the British infantry and artillery in scarlet and blue respectively, the German chasseurs in green coats with red fac-ings and cuffs, the Brunswick dragoons in buff." St. Clair waited, with a force so small, he said, that "had every man I had, been disposed of in single file on the different works, and along the lines of defense, they would have been scarcely within the reach of each other's voices."

Burgoyne disembarked soldiers north of the Ticonderoga/ Independence defenses on both shores on July 4, 1777. Infantry under Friedrich von Riedesel immediately ran into difficulties on the east shore, encountering the long and swampy inlet of East Creek. Thus their mission of cutting off any American retreat was quickly behind schedule. On the west shore, however, Burgoyne's men quickly moved past Ticonderoga and to the slopes of Sugarloaf Hill (later called Mount Defiance). Engineer William Twiss went to the top, came back to report that cannon could indeed be drawn to its 800-foot summit. St. Clair had decided against its fortification, ignoring John Trumbull's and Kosciuszko's advice that it should be manned.

St. Clair was astonished to see British troops on the commanding summit, and on the night of July 5–6, he called a council of war and declared that his fortifications were to be abandoned under the cover of darkness. The plan was for the Ticonderoga troops to cross the lake on a long bridge built the winter before on wood and stone caissons. Most of the army would move south via the military road through upland Hubbardton, and on to Castleton and Skenesborough. Sick and wounded, artillery and supplies, would go by boat to Skenesborough and hence farther south by land. The withdrawal began well enough, in secrecy, but suddenly the whole scene was illuminated for the British when a cabin on The Mount's shore burst into flames. Men stationed at the east end of the bridge to fire a cannon at the approaching British were drunk and never raised a hand, save for another swig. The Americans were in full retreat, over hill and dale and up the lake with the British in close pursuit.

Burgoyne sent a detachment under his trusted lieutenant Simon Fraser to pursue the Americans moving by land. Also in pursuit, though somewhat behind, were Germans under von Riedesel. The Americans made it by darkness on July 6 into the hills above Lake Bomoseen. St. Clair left a rear guard commanded by Seth Warner near the settlement of Hubbardton, on the Castleton Road. Fraser camped that night at the north end of Bomoseen, where the military road turned from the valley to climb steeply into the hills. He had his men up before sunup and just past sunrise the British advance met American pickets where the road passed through the saddle of Sargent Hill. The Americans immediately withdrew, and a battle developed in earnest when Fraser's men reached the American rear guard's camp and a prepared line of battle along Sucker Brook. The Americans fought stubbornly, giving way gradually to the top of a hill, where they made a brief stand. Then with the British advancing, they retreated across the Castleton Road and took position behind a farmer's long log fence. Meanwhile, British soldiers had skirted the American left flank and blocked the Castleton Road. Losses were heavy on both sides, as Americans under another Nathan Hale made an attempt at turning the British right. Historian Bruce Lancaster wrote: "from Fraser's left rear a fearful din arose. Drums boomed, oboes and brass echoed louder, and German voices could be made out, roaring a Lutheran Hymn." Hale's flanking move had itself been flanked by von Riedesel's Brunswickers. The tide of battle had been convincingly turned, and Warner ordered his men to flee east over Pittsford Ridge, to fight again. When it ended, the bloodied grass was still wet with dew. Both sides had suffered fearfully, more than 500 men killed, wounded, or captured. The British dug in at Hubbardton, treating wounded and burying their dead. St. Clair's retreat had been secured, and most of his men, and what remained of Warner's, would indeed fight another day.

Meanwhile, the waterborne escapees from Ticonderoga/Independence had made their way south to Skenesborough (present-day Whitehall, New York). James Thacher, a physician in the Continental army, wrote that "our fleet consisted of five armed gallies and two hundred batteaux and boats deeply laden with cannon, tents, provisions, invalids and women. The night was moonlight and pleasant, the sun burst forth in the morning with uncommon lustre, the day was fine, the water's surface serene and unruffled. At 3 o'clock in the afternoon, we reached our destined port at Skenesborough, being the head of navigation for our gallies. Here we were unsuspicious of danger, but behold! Burgoyne himself was at our heels. In less than 2 hours we were struck with surprise and consternation by a discharge of cannon from the enemy's fleet on our gallies and batteaux lying at the wharf." The doctor continued: "We took the route to Fort Ann through a narrow defile in the woods, and were so closely pressed by the pursuing enemy that we frequently heard calls from the rear to 'march on, the Indians are at our heels.' Having marched all night, we reached Fort Ann at 5 o'clock in the morning, where we found provisions for our refreshment." Dr. Thacher allowed that all baggage, cannon, and several invalids were captured.

The British pressed on. John Burgoyne had driven the rebels from their great stronghold on Lake Champlain, and his veteran army was pointed like a fatal arrow toward the heart of the new nation, straight at New York City. Yet Burgoyne soon learned that the fight in the Vermont hills at Hubbardton had been costlier than first believed. Though Gentleman Johnny, ever publicly the optimist, seemed loathe to admit it, the first serious blow to his great plan for conquest had been dealt at Hubbardton.

St. Clair's army swung east to Rutland, moved south to Manchester, and then west to Fort Edward, where an American force was gathering under Philip Schuyler. While the British pursuit had reached Fort Anne in less than 12 hours, it was met there by American riflemen. After a brief but bloody fight, the British quickly retreated to Skenesborough, making no attempt to hold the advanced post. That allowed Schuyler to take possession of Fort Anne and mount a major effort to delay Burgoyne's expected advance south.

There was reason to think the British might move back to Ticonderoga, and then south via 30-mile-long Lake George, an open and unobstructed avenue. But Burgoyne chose the overland route, via Wood Creek and that rude trail down which the Americans had so swiftly fled to Fort Anne. Schuyler promptly dispatched more than 1,000 men, commanded by John Nixon and including the Green Mountain Rangers under Samuel Herrick, to destroy the road from Skenesborough. This they did by smashing bridges, felling trees, and damming streams. Meanwhile, Burgoyne and his mistress moved into the comfortable home of Philip Skene. Then the British commander sent his army south, bound for Fort Anne some 12 miles distant. The trek would take nearly two weeks. The ground was marshy, and because of all the various obstructions and destroyed bridges, Burgoyne admitted that all he could hear during those trying days was "chop, chop, chop." Forced to build 40 bridges between Skenesborough and Fort Anne, Burgoyne also found that supplies were more of a problem than road obstructions. Writing years later he explained: "In such an undertaking as mine . . . for one hour he (the commander) can find to contemplate how he shall fight his army, he must allot twenty to contrive how to feed it."

Burgoyne reached Fort Anne by the end of July. Then he slogged on toward Fort Edward, arriving there August 11. Needing provisions, since the Americans had been destroying or driving away everything edible, Burgoyne ordered Lt. Col. Friedrich Baum toward Bennington in search of provisions and, perhaps, some arms and powder believed stored there. On August 16, John Stark and 1,500 militia intercepted Baum along the Walloomsac River. Baum immediately went into a defensive position on and around a high hill overlooking the river. Stark responded by ordering a brilliant four-pronged attack. The fighting, according to Stark, lasted two hours and was "the hottest I ever saw. It represented one continuous clap of thunder."

Baum was killed and his entire force smashed, but the battle was not over. Up the muddy road from Cambridge, New York, came British reinforcements under Col. Heinrich Breymann. This could have posed a serious threat to Stark, but in the nick of time Seth Warner arrived from Manchester with reinforcements. Another battle developed; one of Warner's soldiers reporting that his musket became too hot to handle. Darkness ended it, with the British in full retreat, the day having cost them 200 men dead and 700 taken prisoner. The following day, the victors marched triumphantly into Bennington with captives in tow. To the west, Gentleman Johnny was out to greet the remnants of the Bennington expedition as they limped back to camp, congratulating them on their "pretty little success." But he also allowed: "The Hampshire Grants, a country unpeopled and almost unknown in the last war, now abounds in the most active and rebellious race on the continent and hangs like a gathering storm at my left." He would later admit the defeat had been crucial.

JANE McCREA

As Burgoyne struggled south, an event occurred that became the stuff of legend, and which helped rally Americans to oppose the British advance. Along the Hudson just north of Fort Edward, an American woman, Jane McCrea, who happened to be engaged to a Loyalist officer, was killed and scalped, and her bloodstained curls brought into Burgoyne's camp. The Americans blamed the deed on Indians in the employ of the British, though it was said that McCrea had been shot before the scalping. At any rate, "Remember Jane McCrea" became a battle cry of the Americans and added to Burgoyne's worsening woes.

In mid-September, Burgoyne employed a bridge of boats to pass his army from the east to the west bank of the Hudson, intending to force his way to Albany. He did so with the recently acquired knowledge that he would not be joined as planned by Lt. Col. Barry St. Leger; that British colonel had fallen victim, some 100 miles to the west along the Mohawk River, to American forces, which included Benedict Arnold. Also Gen. Henry Clinton, who was supposed to be approaching from New York, had long ago abandoned any such plan, having advanced only a short way up the Hudson. Burgoyne was on his own. He moved southward cautiously, and to the east of Saratoga he confronted a dispiriting sight. On Bemis Heights, overlooking the Hudson where the river plain narrows, American cannon commanded the road, in fortifications that were the work of the brilliant engineer Tadeusz Kosciuszko. Burgoyne had little choice but to attack and the advance came on September 19, with the first of autumn's colors showing on the hills and in the riverside ravines. The British were met by Daniel Morgan's Virginia riflemen, ordered forward by the returned Arnold, in and around the clearing of Freeman's Farm. Morgan struck first, stopping the British advance, but quickly ran into Burgoyne's main line. For three hours the battle raged, the furious musketry blazing through the smoke of cannon fire. In late afternoon, von Riedesel came on with reinforcements and the Americans were forced back to their camp. Though the British claimed victory, the cost had been too high as 500 men lay on the bloodied fields. Burgoyne could stand no more such victories.

Meanwhile, at Burgoyne's rear, fighting broke out again at Fort Ticonderoga and Mount Independence. From Manchester, a detachment under an old friend of Ethan Allen's, Col. John Brown, that included Herrick's Rangers, moved against Fort Ticonderoga. A diversionary attack was made against the British garrison on Mount Independence, while Capt. Ebenezer Allen climbed steep Mount Defiance and sent its British defenders fleeing. Brown then seized all British shipping at Ticonderoga and the northern end of Lake George, and blockhouses at Ticonderoga Falls and at Mount Hope. But his demand that Ticonderoga capitulate was rebuffed by its commander with the words, "The garrison committed to my charge I will defend to the last." Ticonderoga and Mount Independence both proved too well defended to be seized, so Colonel Brown withdrew, taking with him nearly 300 British and Canadian prisoners. He also found and set free 100 American prisoners taken at Hubbardton that he found confined in a barn.

Back on the heights of Saratoga, the balance was swinging increasingly in favor of the Americans; more and more men who had put down plows to grasp weapons were coming in from far and near. The army of American commander Horatio Gates now approached 20,000, while Burgoyne's numbers fell toward 5,000. Growing desperate, the British launched an attack on October 7. But Benedict Arnold, recently relieved of his command by Gates, came on the field to lead a determined American attack. "Arnold rushed into the thickest of the fight with his usual recklessness, and at times acted like a madman," said Capt. Ebenezer Wakefield. "Nothing could exceed the bravery of Arnold on this day. He seemed the very genius of war." Arnold helped turn the battle to the Americans' advantage by personally leading an attack on a British redoubt, though a musket ball smashed into his leg as he jumped his horse over its wall.

British soldier Roger Lamb, who witnessed the fighting, said that "a constant blaze of fire was kept up, and both armies seemed to be determined on death or victory. Men, and particularly officers, dropped every moment on each side. Several of the Americans placed themselves in high trees, and as often as they could distinguish a British officer's uniform, took him off by deliberately aiming at his person."

The wife of Baron von Riedesel was in a farmhouse close behind British lines. "I shivered at every shot," she wrote, "for I could hear everything. I saw a great number of wounded . . . they even brought three of them into the house where I was." Gen. Simon Fraser died in the house.

The British casualties that fateful day were four times more severe than the Americans'. Burgoyne began a retreat north the next day. But he had gone only a few miles when he found his way blocked by Americans on high ground north of Stillwater and on the far bank of the Hudson. The battered British went into a fortified camp above the home of General Schuyler. On October 13, badly outnumbered and with no reinforcements in sight, Burgoyne decided to seek terms of surrender. The formal capitulation took place four days later as the defeated British army marched in perfect order onto a level field along the Hudson to lay down its arms. It would prove to be one of the monumental days in the history of the American nation. As the British regulars trooped onto the field of surrender, having been accorded full military honors by their conquerors, an American band struck up "Yankee Doodle Dandy." The great battle at Saratoga, historians would decide, had been the most decisive of the American Revolution.

Thereafter, the British presence in the Lake Champlain corridor would be minimal and of little strategic importance. Maintaining a base at Point au Fer, north of Plattsburgh, His Majesty's forces occasionally launched raids up Lake Champlain. But the big lake was never again to be fully in British possession. In July 1783, during a lull in fighting, George Washington journeyed north to visit the sites of war he had never seen. He stopped at the old fort at Ticonderoga, and though there is no record that he crossed to Mount Independence, he certainly gazed its way. Then he moved on to Crown Point, where he camped for three days, unaware that the place was still in enemy hands. But the small British garrison was absent and the "Father of His Country" departed safely.

In 1778 Ethan Allen, freed from a British prison in exchange for the man by whom he had been captured, came back to America. He made a triumphant return to Bennington as described in his own words: "I arrived the evening of the last day of May to their great surprise; for I was to them as one rose from the dead and now both their joy and mine was complete. Three cannon were fired that evening, and next morning Col. Herrick gave orders, and fourteen more were discharged welcoming me to Bennington, my usual place of abode, thirteen for the United States, and one for the young Vermont. After this ceremony was ended we moved the flowing bowl, and rural felicity, sweetened with friendship, glowed in each countenance, and with loyal healths to the rising states of America, concluded that evening."

Rare peace descended upon the corridor as the new and independent nation prospered and grew. But storm clouds slowly gathered on the northern horizon, portending a war that would again test the United States' independence. When it came, in 1812, the northern border country blazed with warfare on the Great Lakes and Champlain. Also, the nation's capital was sacked and burned. Great American heroes emerged–Oliver Hazard Perry, Andrew Jackson, and Thomas Macdonough. The war's most famous battle was fought weeks after a peace had been signed, because none of the combatants at New Orleans knew of it. And the war's decisive battle was fought at Plattsburgh, a battle that again thwarted the move south of a mighty British force.

THE WAR OF 1812

The United States declared war on Great Britain on June 18, 1812, a conflict mostly based on matters involving trade and particularly brought on by a British blockade of American shipping. By that time, in a move to protect its northern border country, the federal government had purchased 10 acres atop the bluff overlooking Burlington Harbor as an encampment for its northern army. Late that summer, 28-year-old Thomas Macdonough arrived at Burlington with orders to build a fleet for Lake Champlain. The Delaware native began by refitting a handful of old boats, then moved into Shelburne Harbor, south of Burlington, for the winter with what he called his "forlorn looking squadron." By late fall of that year, 5,000 American troops were camped at Burlington, on the bluff strengthened with earthworks and cannon. Fighting on the lake began early the next summer, in June 1813, when an eager American officer chased some British boats up the Richelieu. Coming under fire from guns on Île-aux-Noix and fighting a hard current, Lt. Sidney Smith lost his two boats and saw more than 100 men taken prisoner.

In July of that year, more than 1,000 British troops crossed the international border and raided Plattsburgh. Accompanying gunboats then crossed the lake to Burlington, where on August 2 they opened fire on the battery. American cannon on the bluff promptly returned fire. The British soon withdrew, but on the way north they landed at Swanton and burned a barracks.

Vermont's militia then moved to Plattsburgh, having volunteered their services to resist any new British invasion. Vermont Governor Martin Chittenden promptly ordered them back, but the soldiers ignored his entreaties, saying it was their duty to protect a sister state's territory. As winter approached, the American northern army again settled in at Burlington. Macdonough took his little fleet south and up Otter Creek to winter under the falls at the manufacturing town of Vergennes. In January 1814, he received orders from President Madison to construct a fleet of 15 warships in order to repel an expected major British invasion of Champlain. Macdonough set to work with supplies coming overland from as far away as Boston, and with iron and timber readily available locally. To protect his shipyard, Macdonough ordered Lt. Stephen Cassin, his second in command, to fortify Otter Creek's mouth. On May 14, the British sailed in and bombarded "Fort Cassin" for nearly two hours. The Americans returned the fire, hitting several ships, and the British withdrew.

Events were building to a climax of battle on land and sea. North of the border, a powerful British army assembled as transports brought from England to Canada seasoned veterans of the Napoleonic Wars. By the autumn of 1814, more than 10,000 men were ready to advance along the lake's west shore. As word of the threat spread through the Champlain Valley, some 2,500 Vermont militiamen headed to Plattsburgh, many of them crossing the shallow Sandbar at Milton on the way. A flotilla of small boats landed most of the Vermonters on the New

York shore. At Plattsburgh, they made up the majority of the 4,500-man army assembled along the fortified south bank of the Saranac River. The British came south from Canada by land and by sea. Historian Hill later wrote: "With the exception of Champlain's battle with the Iroquois and Arnold's desperate encounter at Valcour, the events of September 11, 1814, proved more fateful than any in the history of the lake, and almost as crucial to the destiny of the Union."

The key battle was fought in Plattsburgh Bay by Macdonough's hastily constructed fleet facing a slightly larger British squadron, built on the Richelieu during the winter. Macdonough commanded 11 ships, with 882 men aboard, and 86 guns. The British approached with 16 vessels carrying 937 men and mounting 97 guns. That fleet included the largest warship ever to ply Lake Champlain, the *Confiance*, with at least 36 cannons. As His Majesty's fleet approached Cumberland Head, the Americans could see the tall masts of the British ships beyond the narrow point of land. Macdonough's force was drawn up much as Arnold had arranged his little armada 36 years earlier by nearby Valcour, again forcing the British to attack upwind. One historian wrote: "Crowds of people on Cumberland Head silently watched as the British ships, one by one, their ensigns fluttering in the breeze, took their place opposite the American vessels."

Madonough was aboard his flagship, the *Saratoga*, and years later his grandson described the scene: "There was now a hushed, expectant moment like the stillness which precedes the storm. Macdonough, whose manly courage was supported by a childlike faith, knelt on the deck of the flagship with his officers around him and repeated the prayer appointed by the church to be said before a fight at sea: 'Stir up our strength, oh Lord, and come and help us, for Thou givest not always the battle to the strong, but canst save many or few."

At mid-morning of the brilliant fall day that was September 11, 1814, the fighting began between two fleets largely manned by hastily trained seamen facing their first naval battle. Soon the broadsides were coming fast and furious. Macdonough worked guns alongside his sailors. Twice the impact of shells sent him to the deck; then a shot beheaded a gunner, driving the lifeless head against the commodore, knocking him senseless for a brief time. The decks were bloodied as dead and wounded lay everywhere.

At 11:20 AM, the British struck their colors. The battle had lasted less than two-and-one-half hours. Macdonough wrote: "I could only look at the enemy's galleys going off in a shattered condition; for there was not a mast in either squadron that could stand to make sail on." The Americans were victorious, but had lost 52 men, with 58 wounded. The British toll was 54 dead, 116 wounded. The British officers came to the *Saratoga* for the formal surrender, offering their swords. But Macdonough refused their weapons because, he said, they were "worthy of them." The dead of both sides were taken to little Crab Island, in the middle of the bay, for burial in a common grave; afterwards a formal military ceremony was attended by officers and men of both sides.

On land, the British army had moved to the north bank of the Saranac River, ready to launch their seasoned veterans against the badly outnumbered Americans in their fortifications. The Americans waited in defenses keyed to three large earthen forts. The British commander ordered a crossing of the river at three points. Two attempts were made within the village of Plattsburgh, and both were repulsed. However, those attacks were only a feint as the main British land effort came well upstream along the Saranac, to the west. After crossing the river at Fredenburgh Falls, the British moved uphill and into the sandy scrub pine hills south of the river. There New York militia opened fire, stubbornly giving way. Then the British were hit by heavier fire, from Vermonters and American regulars, laying in ambush. As the fight increased in intensity, British commander Sir George Prevost heard shouts of victory from his foes, as they had just been told of the surrender of the giant *Confiance*. He wrote: "This unlooked for event depriving me of the cooperation of the Fleet without which the further prosecution of the service was become impracticable, I did not hesitate to arrest the course of the troops advancing to attack." The British, no doubt having in mind Burgoyne's fate, ceased firing and withdrew, bound for Canada. An American band bid them farewell with "Yankee Doodle Dandy," and Macdonough dashed off a message to the War Department in Washington that read: "Sir, the Almighty has been pleased to grant us a signal victory on Lake Champlain in the capture of one frigate, one brig and two sloops of war of the enemy."

Macdonough sailed his battered fleet, along with the captured and splintered British vessels, south to Whitehall. On the way, the flagship *Saratoga* and the captured *Confiance* sailed close to Burlington on October 2, saluted by cannon on the battery. As historian Hill noted, it was "the last time big guns ever spoke on Lake Champlain." The victorious fleet and its captive vessels anchored just north of Whitehall, where they rested at the mouth of East Bay awaiting another call to action. It never came. The War of 1812 ended the following Christmas. Over the years the historic ships slowly settled to the murky depths.

In 1816, the U.S. government began construction, on the New York shore just south of the Canadian border, of a large stone fortification intended to stop, once and for all, any British incursions up the lake. Then came the startling discovery that the fort was being built on the Canadian side of the border. The fortification quickly assumed the lasting sobriquet of Fort Blunder. With the signing of the Webster/Ashburton Treaty in 1842, the fort's site deed was given to the United States. Work was begun on a much larger structure, and it was after the Civil War that work was completed on a massive new bastion named Fort Montgomery, whose walls still stand along the border waters.

Before the Civil War, some citizens of the corridor became involved in helping escaped slaves from the south make their way to freedom in Canada. While countless houses along the corridor claim to have been Underground Railroad stops, much of the truth has been lost, and such claims are difficult to prove. But there can be no doubt that one historic structure, Rokeby, home of the Quaker Robinson family in Ferris-burgh, Vermont, was an Underground Railroad stop. Correspondence exists in Robinson family archives between escaped slaves and their Quaker former hosts. One such letter is from James Temple, once a slave, then living a free man in Montréal:

> I am at work at my trade getting a living looking through the glasses you gave me for which I never shall forget to be thankful I am working for Mr. Harding No 111 main street I think I shall soon be able to send for my family if I conclude to stay here. Please remember me to your colored people . . . I shall never forget you and all your kindness to me may the peace of god keep you until the day of your deliverance.

JOHN BROWN

The slavery issue had burned hot along the corridor, but nowhere more so than in the high Adirondacks at North Elba, where, in 1855, John Brown and his large and growing family had settled in the shadow of Whiteface Mountain amid a colony of free blacks. That year, Brown journeyed to Kansas and became deeply involved in the fighting be-tween pro-slavery and anti-slavery forces. Returning to North Elba, Brown was a familiar figure on both sides of the northern part of the lake, sometimes coming to Vergennes, Vermont, via ferry to do his trading. In 1859, he set off south from the Adirondacks, determined to start a slave uprising. With a small band of supporters, Brown de-scended on Harpers Ferry, Virginia, on October 16 to seize weapons from the federal arsenal there. U.S. troops under Robert E. Lee were quickly called in, and Brown and what remained of his battered little band were surrounded and captured. The wounded Brown was promptly tried and sentenced to death. Before leaving his cell for the gallows, Brown handed his jailer a note that said, "I, John Brown, am quite certain that the crimes of this guilty land will never be purged away but with blood." John Brown's body came by train along the Champlain Valley to Vergennes, was taken across the lake on the ferry at Arnold's Bay, then borne on its slow way back into the mountains for burial in his North Elba farmyard.

The Harpers Ferry raid incensed the Southern states, and a year and a half later, the Civil War erupted with the firing upon Fort Sumter in Charleston Harbor, South Carolina. The fighting was mainly far away from the Champlain Corridor, until a day in October 1864 when it broke out in a busy Vermont town not far from Lake Champlain's shore and the Canadian border. By then, with the war deep in its fourth year, the Confederacy was on the defensive. At Petersburg, Ulysses S. Grant had Robert E. Lee's once mighty army under siege and Gen. William Tecumseh Sherman had seized Atlanta and was about to begin his drive to the sea. In St. Albans, Vermont, as the leaves faded, a score of young strangers posing as workmen began drifting into town, taking rooms in local hotels. They were, in fact, Confederate soldiers escaped from Yankee prison pens who had in recent months made their way to Montréal. On October 19, their leader, Bennett Young of Kentucky, and his men took up arms and robbed St. Albans' three banks of $208,000 dollars. Escaping from a hail of gunfire to Canada, part of the raiding party was captured north of the border. But in a trial of extradition held in Montréal, a judge ruled that the Confederates could remain free on British soil. The St. Albans Raid was the northernmost land action of the war, and it resulted in a panic that for some time gripped the North Country. Troops under Vermonter George Stannard, one of the heroes of Gettysburg, were moved to the border. But Confederates never again ventured across the international line, and in the spring of 1865 the nation was again united, and at peace.

So the guns were silent, and there our story ends. This book concerns military sites along the corridor associated with wars up to, and including, the Civil War. Of course, war would again touch the area. In later years, a large military base, Fort Ethan Allen, was built near Burlington, and among those who manned it were the storied Buffalo Soldiers. The Plattsburgh military base continued to operate until 1995, in its later years as an air force base. Nuclear missiles were stored in silos at a dozen sites in the Plattsburgh area and nuclear bombs, ready for transport by ever-present B-47 and B-52 bombers, were held in readiness on the base. Atop a high hill overlooking St. Albans, giant white domes housing radar were constructed, keeping an electronic eye to the north, not for the British, but for Soviet planes and missiles. But the bombers and bombs now are gone and the radar domes stand unused, though National Guard jets still roar aloft out of Burlington reminding that the world is far from being at peace. Along the upper Hudson and Richelieu, Lake George and Lake Champlain, many of the ramparts of long-ago conflicts still stand, and the dead of Fort William Henry and Ticonderoga, Bennington, Hubbardton, Saratoga, and Plattsburgh rest in the famous soil, remembered for their deeds in an earlier time of *Guns Over the Champlain Valley*.

Chapter Two

Saratoga

To BEGIN A TOUR of the Champlain Corridor at the Saratoga Battlefield is much like playing a great symphony in reverse, to begin, say, Beethoven's *Ninth Symphony* with the "Ode to Joy." All that would come after might seem anticlimactic. Yet we do begin with Saratoga, for it is the southern entrance to the region and far more people live to the south than to the north. And this corridor is so rich in important sites that any feeling of disappointment at having experienced the major site first will quickly be dispelled on encountering the other important historic places that await the visitor. Saratoga is probably the corridor's most important historic site, scene of the six-week-long confrontation generally known as the Battle of Saratoga, the decisive conflict of the American Revolution. The battlefield has been restored to its appearance at the time of the battle, old woods are once again woods, old fields are once again fields. One building, the Neilson House, still stands as it did amid the fray. Long rows of colored stakes mark the long British and American lines. Cannon stand at the strategic places where American engineers positioned their strongpoints to stop Burgoyne's southward drive. Corner stakes denote the location of the Taylor farmhouse where Baroness von Riedesel survived and wrote of the great battle, and in which Gen. Simon Fraser died. Great trees that may have witnessed the fighting keep their vigil in a remote part of the battlefield. Throughout the storied acreage, one still observes the clear course

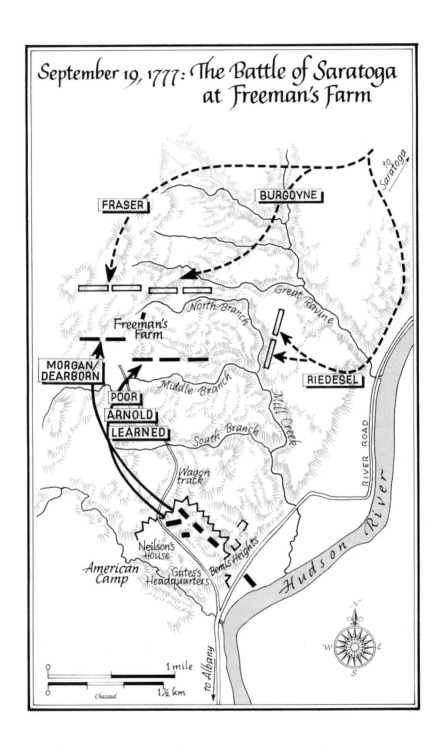

September 19, 1777: The Battle of Saratoga at Freeman's Farm

FRASER

BURGOYNE

to Saratoga

Great Ravine

North Branch

Freeman's Farm

RIEDESEL

MORGAN/
DEARBORN

Middle Branch

Mill Creek

POOR

ARNOLD

LEARNED

South Branch

RIVER ROAD

Wagon
track

Neilson's
House

American
Camp

Gates's
Headquarters

Bemis Heights

Hudson River

N

W   E

S

1 mile

Chazaud

½ km

to Albany

of roads used by the armies of Gates and Burgoyne. At the Visitors Center you can still view cannon captured from the defeated British.

Directions

The Saratoga National Historical Park may be reached by following signs from I-87, the Northway, on approaching Saratoga Springs from the north or south. Or, there's an entrance to the park on US 4 along the Hudson River, just south of Schuylerville.

The Visitors Center is open daily 9–5 all year, except Thanksgiving, Christmas, and New Year Year's Day. The tour road that leads throughout the battlefield closes when snow makes it unsafe, but otherwise is open year-round. Admission fee.

After the defeat of Burgoyne's foraging expedition toward Bennington, on August 16, 1777, he continued farther south, bound for Albany, where he hoped to meet reinforcements. But on September 3 came news that St. Leger had been turned back from the Mohawk River. Thus, there was ever more reason for the British commander to be concerned, for Burgoyne was still alone and time was limited, the nights' chill foretelling winter. Perhaps it was time to turn back, but orders were orders and his told him to proceed to Albany. So Burgoyne moved down the Hudson, and, on September 13, he cut his communications with Canada by crossing to the west bank near Saratoga. Then he continued his slow way south, continually harassed by American skirmishers, coming down the rough road beside the widening river. Meanwhile, Philip Schuyler decided it was time for his American forces to stop retreating, time to turn and face the enemy. His delaying tactics, employed all the way from Skenesborough, had been most effective. Yet, far from being praised, Congress removed Schuyler from command of the northern army. He, like Arthur St. Clair, would face a court martial for having abandoned Ticonderoga/Independence. Cautious Horatio Gates, a former British officer, was then given command of the northern army.

On September 8, General Gates moved his headquarters from the town of Stillwater and camped on Bemis Heights behind long fortifications skillfully placed by Tadeusz Kosciuszko. A battery anchored the American line on a bluff overlooking the Hudson, effectively blocking the river road. If the British were to continue southward, they would have to move against the Americans occupying a commanding and fortified position. Gates gave Benedict Arnold command of the American left wing, made up of the New York and Connecticut militia, New Hampshire regulars, and Daniel Morgan's seasoned riflemen from Virginia. Gates himself commanded the right wing, while James Livingston's New Yorkers and Ebenezer Learned's Massachusetts troops held the center.

The entrenched Americans awaited Burgoyne's move. It came on September 19, under the watchful eyes of American scouts concealed in trees. Having placed his supplies and hospital on the riverside flats behind him, Burgoyne followed cart paths up through the woods and onto a plateau to the west. His intent was to smash through the American resistance and move on to Albany, and to do so he divided his force into three sections. Baron von Riedesel led his troops and artillery on the river road, Burgoyne himself commanded the center, while Simon Fraser, supported by Colonel Breymann, commanded the right, aiming to turn the American left.

General Gates had planned to wait behind his breastworks and, hopefully, let Burgoyne break his army in assaults against them. But Benedict Arnold had other plans. Ever aggressive, Arnold argued for an attack and, reluctantly, Gates allowed him to move Morgan and his riflemen forward toward an abandoned farm, a mile north of the American camp, owned by a man named Freeman. Suddenly, out into the fields came the first wave of soldiers in faded scarlet. Morgan's long rifles fired and holes opened in the British line of battle. British losses immediately were significant, with many officers cut down by the American marksmen. The firing eased, then resumed with heightened intensity.

Morgan's initial attack had run into the center of Burgoyne's line, and for three hours the battle raged back and forth across Freeman's trampled field of wheat. Burgoyne stood in the midst of it, hat and coat pierced with bullets, urging on his men until out of the woods, on his left, came von Riedesel to turn the tide. The Americans left the field to a badly battered enemy. Though Gentleman Johnny claimed victory, it had cost him 500 men.

The two armies dug in and, for two weeks, improved their defenses. The Americans were filled with confidence for they had, after all, attacked the king's professional army and its mercenaries and held their own. They were more than willing to fight again. Burgoyne strengthened his works, which included the Breymann Redoubt, the Balcarres Redoubt, and, on the edge of the plateau overlooking the river, the Great Redoubt. Two days after the September 19 battle, Burgoyne received a message from Sir Henry Clinton saying that he was about to attack Forts Montgomery and Clinton on the Hudson. Burgoyne asked him to hurry, for he could last only until mid-October before being forced back on Ticonderoga. Slow-moving Clinton did take Fort Montgomery and Fort Clinton, but he came no farther north. As the American numbers grew, the British faced an increasingly dispiriting situation. Morgan's sharpshooters took a continuing toll on unwary soldiers and men grew gaunt as rations of flour and salt pork were reduced, then reduced again. Horses starved on a diet of leaves.

In the American camp, the fiery Arnold had fallen afoul of Horatio Gates. Heated words were exchanged when Gates failed to credit Arnold's part in the battle at Freeman's Farm. Gates responded by stripping Arnold of his command and excluding him from headquarters. In his place, Benjamin Lincoln was given command of the American left wing. On October 7, drums rolled again as, with 1,500 men, Burgoyne began a reconnaissance in force, again directed at the left of the American line. American James Wilkinson watched through his glass, then reported to Gates, "I think, sir, they are offering you battle . . . I would indulge them." "Very well," replied Gates, "order on Morgan to begin the game." The Americans met the British advance powerfully, sending the British back to their redoubts. Burgoyne, Fraser, and von Riedesel were again on the field, attempting to slow the retreat. Burgoyne's uniform was again riddled and, suddenly, Fraser reeled in the saddle, mortally wounded by a shot reportedly fired by Tim Murphy, one of Morgan's riflemen.

As British resistance stiffened, Arnold asked Gates's permission to join the fray. Reluctantly, it was given and Arnold mounted a borrowed horse and was off, sweeping up two brigades. Arnold flung them against the Balcarres Redoubt, but failing to carry it, he rode through the fire of both sides to the Breymann Redoubt. There, he joined the final onslaught that overwhelmed the position. In the victorious assault, Arnold was shot in the leg and carried from the field. Had the wound been mortal, he would have died a hero that day, perhaps a hero ever after to the young nation.

During the afternoon, in a cabin at the base of the bluffs, Madame von Riedesel had prepared dinner, expecting to host her husband and other officers. Instead, she wrote: "About three o'clock in the afternoon they brought in to me upon a litter poor General Fraser . . . Our dining table which was already spread was taken away and in its place they fixed up a bed for the general." Told that his wound was mortal, Fraser

The Great Redoubt

sent a message to Burgoyne asking to be buried at six the next evening atop a bluff overlooking the Hudson. At eight the next morning Fraser died and, that evening, with full military honors, the general was buried in the fortifications of the Great Redoubt, to the unwanted accompaniment of an American cannonade.

That night, in the rain, leaving campfires burning, Burgoyne began his retreat. It led only 8 miles, to a ridgetop. Burgoyne dug in there, having encountered American forces, including men under John Stark, blocking his way north toward Ticonderoga. The British commander could not bear the word "capitulation," and as it was the custom of military code that the vanquished propose terms, Burgoyne instead offered a "convention." Gates accepted, and on October 17 the tired British troops marched to a field alongside the Hudson and stacked arms. On Gates's order, no Americans were present to watch the British humiliation.

James Wilkinson escorted Burgoyne to meet the American commander. "General Gates, advised of Burgoyne's approach," Wilkinson wrote, "met him at the head of his camp, Burgoyne in a rich royal uniform and Gates in a plain blue frock. When they approached nearly within a sword's length they reined up and halted and I then named the gentleman, and General Burgoyne, raising his hat most gracefully, said, "'The fortunes of war, General Gates, have made me your prisoner,' to which the conqueror, returning to a courtly salute, promptly replied, "'I shall always be ready to bear testimony, that it has not been through any fault of your Excellency.'" Then side by side the two commanders watched the unarmed British army march by. Burgoyne then drew his sword and, without a word, handed it to Gates who took it with a bow and returned it. Later, back in London, Burgoyne, reflecting on the last battle, said it was Arnold who turned the tide.

Touring Saratoga

Visitors Center

Tens of thousands of people from throughout the world visit the Saratoga National Historical Park each year at its majestic setting on the high ground above the historic Hudson. The Visitors Center, the location of which is said to have been chosen by Franklin Delano Roosevelt, commands a fine view of the battlefield, and offers a film on the Burgoyne campaign and its final battles. Among the exhibits are two of the four medium 12-pounder cannon that Burgoyne brought with him to Saratoga (the museum owns all four) and a cufflink initialed "JB" that likely belonged to Burgoyne. From the Visitors Center a paved road winds through the 5,300-acre park along which there are 12 stops. A tape-recorded auto tour is available. Also, hiking trails wind through the park, sometimes following the course of roads once used by the armies. The auto tour includes the following stops:

Stop 1 Freeman Farm Overlook: The view is across much of the battlefield to the distant, still-open fields of the Loyalist John Freeman's farm, where savage fighting occurred on September 19 and October 7, and the Barber Wheat Field.

Stop 2 Neilson Farm. The Neilson House, home of John Neilson who fought with the Americans, looks much as it did at the time of the battle. The building, once used as quarters by American officers, likely including Benedict Arnold, is on a height known at the time of the battle as "The Summit." The Americans made a strongpoint in their fortifications here. From the house, you will see long lines of white stakes topped in blue marking the American lines, and white stakes topped with red marking the British position. Also visible some distance to the south is the location of General Gates's headquarters and of the American hospital, both of which have been excavated and will, one day, be interpreted and added to the tour.

Stop 3 American River Fortifications. Artillery still stands atop the bluffs where engineer Kosciuszko raised earthworks to command the river valley and road. These fortifications stopped Burgoyne's advance toward Albany and forced him to attack the Americans in their high-sited positions.

Stop 4 Chatfield Farm. American pickets posted on this ridge spotted the British advance that began the battle on October 7.

Stop 5 Barber Wheat Field. Here, on October 7, the Americans intercepted the 1,500 British and German soldiers advancing to turn

The Neilson Farm, Saratoga National Park

the American left. A painting of the battle makes clear the astonishing length of the battle lines. A short paved path leads to a small monument marking the spot where Simon Fraser fell.

Stop 6 The Balcarres Redoubt. This stop on the Freeman Farm was fought over during the battles of September 19 and October 7. Freeman's house stood on the ridge where the Balcarres Redoubt was built. To orient yourself concerning the September fight, walk from the parking lot to the large cannon nearby. The cannon is along the British line of battle that Burgoyne directed into the Freeman field to encounter Morgan's long rifles, soon supported by additional troops. The Americans emerged from the woods to the front, where the cannon is aimed. The fighting raged back and forth across this field until von Riedesel appeared from the woods on the left, or east, to deliver the sudden flank attack that drove the Americans from the field. On October 7, the Americans attacked, but failed to capture, the formidable fortifications of the Balcarres Redoubt, located on a low ridge and named for the commander of the British light infantry, Alexander Lindsay, Earl of Balcarres. A path runs along the ground where the redoubt once stood, to Bloody Knoll to the front, where vicious fighting took place.

Stop 7 The Breymann Redoubt. Named for the commander of the German troops, this 200-yard-long breastwork guarding the British right flank was overrun by the Americans on October 7. Benedict Arnold helped lead the attack and a monument stands on the spot where he was wounded. The famous "leg monument" honors the hero of Saratoga, soon to become a traitor, without mentioning his name.

Stop 8 Burgoyne's Headquarters. A path leads to the spot where Burgoyne sited his headquarters, near a clear spring, after the September 19 battle. The spring, incidentally, still provides water for the visitors center. The surrounding fields were filled with the tents of British regulars.

Stop 9 The Great Redoubt. Here British cannon protected Burgoyne's supplies and hospital, located at the base of the bluff. The view is across the Hudson River valley and New York hills to the Green Mountains of Vermont, a broad and beautiful American landscape. Here one sees the prize for which more than 20,000 men battled in the late summer and early autumn of 1777. The prize, quite simply, was America.

Stop 10 Fraser Burial Site and Trail. A path leads to the base of the bluffs and the site of the Taylor House, where Baroness von Riedesel lodged and where the wounded Fraser was taken to die. Fraser asked to be buried in the Great Redoubt, and his wish was fulfilled. Burgoyne attended the burial, as American cannon sent shells toward the blufftop. On the high ground where the trail begins it is said that, from time to time, a figure clad in a British uniform is seen at 1 AM. Fraser's remains have never been found, and it is reported that they may have been exhumed and taken back to Britain.

Directions
Depart the Saratoga Battlefield by the east entrance and immediately turn north on US 4. Just over 5.5 miles along, on the right side by two small houses, is a marker at the site of General Gates's headquarters prior to Burgoyne's surrender. Continue north 0.75 mile and note, on the left, a marker on private property where the surrender took place. Continue north 0.5 mile and on your right is the Schuyler House.

SCHUYLER HOUSE

General Philip Schuyler's original home, on this site, was burned by the British on October 10, 1777, to prevent the Americans from using it for cover during Burgoyne's final encampment on the heights above. Only the outhouse was spared, which still stands behind the main house.

The Schuyler House is open Wednesday through Sunday, from Memorial Day to Labor Day 9:30–4:30. No admission fee.

Schuyler began construction of this new home three weeks after Burgoyne's surrender, and the British commander offered the help of his soldiers in return for Schuyler's kind treatment of prisoners. The house contains period furnishings and items that belonged to Schuyler. The building's color, "English ivory," was popular in the late 18th century.

Philip Schuyler House at Schuylerville

Visitors here have included George Washington, Alexander Hamilton, and the Marquis de Lafayette.

Directions

Continue north on US 4 and immediately on entering the village of Schuylerville, turn left on Burgoyne Street. At the top of the hill is the Saratoga Monument.

SARATOGA MONUMENT

The ornate 155-foot-high monument located on the site of Burgoyne's final headquarters commemorates the surrender of Burgoyne's army. Completed in 1883, three statues of American heroes stand in niches; Schuyler faces east, Gates north, and Daniel Morgan west, the southern niche is empty, testa-

Open Memorial Day to Labor Day, Wednesday through Sunday, 9:30–4:30. No admission fee.

ment to Benedict Arnold's treachery. The 200-step climb brings you to a gallery that offers fine views.

Directions
Return down the hill, turn north on US 4, and at the stoplight turn right onto NY 29. Turn into Fort Hardy Park, which is a complex of athletic fields.

FORT HARDY PARK

In these fields beside the Hudson River, the British stacked arms before marching off to surrender. The British built a fort here in 1757, though nothing of it remains. The small Visitors Center in the park has a model of Fort Hardy and information about the British surrender.

Fort Hardy is open in the summer; call 518-563-7702 for further information.

Chapter Three

The Battle of Bennington

THE MARCH TOWARD BENNINGTON

Directions

Leaving Fort Hardy Park, turn east, or left, on NY 29 and follow it 5 miles through Middle Falls to the center of Greenwich, then take NY 372 for 9 miles to Cambridge, New York.

Though the British in 1777 had referred to the country through which they passed as a "swampy forest," today the beauty of the landscape between the Hudson River and the Vermont border known now as "Grandma Moses Country," is most impressive. Yet this hilly land of fields, farms, and gentle valleys clearly was ominous country to British and German soldiers, deep in hostile country and headed toward an uncertain fate. Opinions differ today on just where Baum and Breymann left Burgoyne's main column. Most accounts point to Fort Miller, though others indicate Fort Edward, and some the mouth of the Batten Kill. At any rate, once Cambridge is reached, there is little doubt how the columns marched; from there to the battlefield, you'll follow Baum and Breymann's route.

Directions

Proceed south along what is now NY 22 and then east on NY 67. Approaching the old village of North Hoosick, called Sancoick at the time

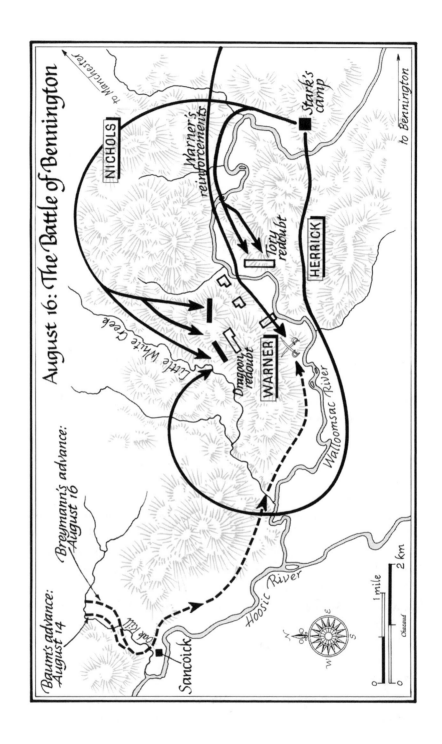

August 16: The Battle of Bennington

NICHOLS

Warner's reinforcements

Tory redoubt

HERRICK

Dragoon redoubt

WARNER

Little White Creek

Stark's camp

to Manchester

to Bennington

Walloomsac River

Baum's advance: August 14

Breymann's advance: August 16

Van Kill

Sancoick

Hoosic River

N

W E

S

0 1 mile

0 2 km

Chazaud

of the battle, look for a small stone marker on the right, just before the NORTH HOOSICK sign. It notes that, near that spot, Baum wrote his famous letter "on the head of a barrel." Continue on for 2.5 miles, and on the left you'll see the sign at the entrance to the Bennington Battlefield. You may want to pull into the entrance to read the following story of the battle, but wait before driving to the hilltop.

THE BATTLE OF BENNINGTON

"About twenty miles to the eastward of the Hudson lies the obscure village of Bennington," wrote a Hessian officer named Gilch, "a poor cluster of cottages situated in a wild country between the forks of the Hoosac. Here the enemy had gathered together a considerable depot of cattle, cows, horses and wheel carriages, most of which were drawn across the Connecticut River from the provinces of New England; and as it was understood to be guarded by a part of militia only, an attempt to surprise it seemed by no means unjustifiable." As Burgoyne moved deeper into hostile country, he grew ever more short of supplies and horses. To remedy this, he dispatched from the vicinity of Fort Miller 500 men commanded by Lt. Col. Friedrich von Baum, bound in the direction of Bennington, where a substantial cache of American military supplies was said to be stored. Off into the wilds they went, to Cambridge and on to a hamlet then known as Sancoick along the Walloomsac River. An officer wrote that he saw but "one prodigious forest, bottomed in swamps and morasses." Things worsened when the advance of the column had a brief skirmish at Cambridge, a handful of prisoners were taken who reported that 1,500 American troops were at Bennington. Still, Baum pushed on to Sancoick, where he encountered more American skirmishers. There he dashed off a message to Burgoyne, asking for reinforcements. About that time, John Stark had set forth from Bennington with 1,500 troops, mostly from New Hampshire but also including Vermonters and Massachusetts men. Baum pressed on, along the valley of the Walloomsac and, encountering militia, he entrenched to await reinforcements. By darkness, on August 14, Stark's full force was in sight across the river.

Baum centered his deployment where a bridge carried the Bennington Road across the Walloomsac. There he erected breastworks on the river's west side, posted men in cabins on the eastern bank, and covered the position with two small cannon set in an earthwork above the bridge. On a ridge overlooking the position, south and east on the far bank of the river, Baum had some 200 local British Loyalists construct a small fortification known as the Tory Redoubt. The biggest fortification was built atop the high hill rising abruptly from the river west of the bridge. A large three-sided redoubt was constructed of logs, facing west, toward the only side of the hill that did not drop precipitously away. On that western side, the land ran away fairly level toward higher ground. Also, Baum placed 50 men in a small earthwork on the hill's northern side to guard against a flank attack.

Rain fell all the day of August 15 preventing a major clash, though Stark harassed Baum with skirmishers, inflicting casualties, in sorties from the American camp. Baum's men spent the day improving defenses, especially strengthening the large hilltop position. Meanwhile, Burgoyne dispatched reinforcements under Col. Heinrich Breymann to Baum's aid and some 500 troops were soon struggling along the muddy roads previously tramped by Baum's men.

After the long rains, August 16 dawned clear and hot. "Innumerable raindrops glistened on the forest, grass-lands, fields of corn, and ripening wheat," wrote the historian Rowland Robinson. "Clouds of rising vapor were glorified in the level sunbeams that turned the turbid reaches of the swollen Walloomsac to a beat of gold." Stark launched his attack that afternoon and the strategy was a complex one, a four-pronged offensive directed against the bridge fortifications, the Tory Redoubt, the small redoubt, and the hilltop redoubt. In the morning, Stark had sent two columns on long marches, one to the north and one to the south, to reach the high ground fronting the hilltop position's western side. Colonel Moses Nichols, with 200 New Hampshire men, circled Baum's right by moving well down the Walloomsac before crossing and moving up into the hills. To the north, Col. Samuel Herrick, with 300 Vermonters, also crossed the river and tramped to high ground circling Baum's left. By mid-afternoon both commands were in position in the woods near the hilltop redoubt. Stark attacked about 3 PM and tradition says that as he did so he roared, "There are the Redcoats and they are ours, or this night Molly Stark sleeps a widow," words that have joined in American legend such pronouncements as "Don't fire 'til you see the whites of their eyes," and "Damn the torpedoes and straight ahead." Though Stark outnumbered his entrenched foe by at least two to one, the complex assault at Bennington must be regarded as an ingenious bit of military workmanship. Somehow, in a time before walkie-talkies, Nichols and Herrick advanced against the hilltop redoubt at almost the same time that the Tory Redoubt was assaulted and that Stark led the attack at the bridge. The Tory Redoubt fell promptly, as the Americans discovered a ravine leading past the position's south side through which they moved undetected. Then they attacked up a steep embankment in the rear of the startled Tories who fired one volley and fled. Stark, after what must have been a brief and furious fight, overwhelmed the British at the bridge, mortally wounding Baum in the process and capturing the one cannon firing from the hillside position. The other had been moved that day to the hilltop redoubt. Up there, Herrick and Nichols attacked simultaneously and within the stronghold the veteran German soldiers put up a fierce resistance.

"We were surrounded on all sides; columns were everywhere advancing against us," said German soldier Gilch, who wrote: "In general it lasted 2 hours, the hottest I ever saw in my life. It represented one continuous clap of thunder." Stark, it should be noted, had previously experienced the fury of Bunker Hill and Abercromby's doomed assault on Carillon. A farmer living nearby likened the rifle fire to the snapping of brush in a bonfire. Baum's dragoons fought to the last, wielding sabers as their position was overrun. When at last they fled, the Americans pursued them downhill, killing many and taking most of the rest as prisoners. The victory seemed complete, and historian Rowland Robinson later wrote that "the militia dispersed over the blood-stained field in quest of spoil. But they were brought together again by the alarm that another British force was coming up, and was only two miles away. The rattle of their drums and the screech of their fifes could be heard shaking and piercing the sultry air. It was Breymann's force of German veterans."

Quickly, Herrick and Stark managed to round up a sufficient number of men to move a mile west and, by a mill along the Walloomsac, meet the advancing force. But they were soon driven back, almost to the bridge, by superior numbers and British cannon. At that moment of crisis, as if scripted for an old Western movie in which the cavalry rides over the hill, reinforcements under Seth Warner, marching down from Manchester, reached the field. Stark said, "Lucky for us, that moment Colonel Warner's regiment came up fresh, who marched on and began the attack afresh . . . I pushed forward as many of the men as I could to their assistance. The battle continued obstinate on both sides till sunset. The enemy was obliged to retreat. We pursued them till dark. But had daylight lasted one hour longer, we should have taken the whole body of them." Stark claimed 700 prisoners and four brass cannon were captured. More than 200 of the enemy were dead. American losses, he said, were 40 wounded and 30 dead. The prisoners were marched off to Bennington. Philip Lord, in his remarkable book on the battle and battlefield, wrote:

> That confrontation, which lasted less than 48 hours, is believed by many to have been the death knell of the Burgoyne invasion. The failure of Baum's expedition, coupled with the loss of support from Howe and St. Leger, directly contributed to the defeat of the main British force at Stillwater a few weeks later. Most historians believe this battle turned the tide of the Revolution and was one of the most significant battles in the history of the world.

At Bennington, Stark had done to Baum something very much like Crazy Horse and Gall would do to Custer a century later. Though the sudden approach of Breymann could have spoiled Stark's glorious day, the fortunes of war brought Warner on the scene at just the right time. Incidentally, Warner's brother Jesse was killed in the fight. Back along the Hudson, Burgoyne greeted Breymann's battered column and the few escapees from Baum's force with cheery words and praise. But he well knew the cost of his failed Bennington expedition had been high.

Touring the Battlefield of Bennington

Directions
Leave the park entrance, then continue east on NY 67, and quickly note, on the right, the CARETAKER'S ROAD sign. Go past the sign for 2

miles and then turn right onto Harrison Road. Follow it uphill 0.75 mile until you see, in the field on the left, a stone marker at the site of John Stark's camp. From here, Stark launched his attacks on August 16. Also, Seth Warner paused here before moving out to fight Breymann's supporting column. Turn around and return to NY 67 and drive back to Caretaker's Road. Drive down it and park where it ends at an old bridge that spans the Walloomsac. This is the site of the bridge that was the center of Baum's position and the focus of Stark's attack. On the near side, where you stand, Baum threw up entrenchments and fought from within them. Some of his troops also were sheltered in cabins that stood just across the river. Baum was mortally wounded in this area, probably in a field along the river off behind where the large brick house now stands. A cannon on the hill behind supported the position. Look across the river, to the front and right, and the ridge rising beyond the trees was the site of the Tory Redoubt. Clearly, Baum had to fortify that ridge as it commanded his river position. Return to NY 67, turn left, and quickly turn right into the New York State–owned Bennington Battlefield. Drive to the parking lot at the top of the hill.

BENNINGTON BATTLEFIELD

You are now in the battlefield park, owned by the State of New York, which encompasses but a portion of the 1777 battlefield. On reaching the hilltop parking lot, you are within the area encompassed by the British hilltop redoubt. Walk to the high point nearby and from this 863-foot-high summit a wonderful view unfolds to the Green Mountains of Vermont and Massachusetts's Berkshires. When the leaves are gone, the grand Bennington Battle Monument in Bennington is clearly visible. At the hill's highest point is a relief map of the surrounding countryside and large diagrams explaining the battle. Here you stand at the center of Baum's redoubt, the scene of the last desperate struggle, some of

The Bennington Battlefield is open 9 AM to dusk, year-round. However, the road to the battlefield is open only during the warm months. If the gate is closed, a brisk 10–15 minute uphill walk brings you to the summit.

it hand to hand. Along the sides of the hill are monuments to Stark and his New Hampshire men and to soldiers from Massachusetts and Vermont. The focus of your attention should be to the west, where the road enters the highest parking lot. Walk across the lot and through the screen of trees on the little road and into the field beyond. It was from this direction that the forces of Nichols and Herrick struck the redoubt, attacking over relatively level ground, avoiding a suicidal uphill attack that an assault on the other sides of the position would have produced. You may also want to visit the small Visitors Center, by the picnic area, which also interprets the battle.

Directions

Returning to NY 67, turn left and 3 miles along, after crossing the Vermont border, look for a marker near the site of the house where the wounded Baum died. There is no turnoff by the marker. Continue on VT 67 into the village of North Bennington and take VT 67A, soon picking up VT 7A south. Follow VT 7A to Benmont Road, marked by a large overhead sign, and turn right onto it and in 1 mile reach its intersection with VT 9. Turn west on VT 9 and go up the hill toward Old Bennington. Turn left at the top of the hill and park by the white Old First Church on the left.

OLD BENNINGTON

Old Bennington and its stately, shaded Monument Avenue may well be the most historic place in Vermont. The south end of the avenue is dominated by the graceful Old First Church, which opened for worship in 1806. The church contains box pews and the soaring pulpit of a classic New England meetinghouse. From the church, cross the road to the small green and see the low monument marking the location of the church's predecessor, the first Protestant church organized in Vermont. Some 700 British and German prisoners were brought to Bennington after the battle and kept under guard in that old meetinghouse. Also within the building, on January 10, 1791, delegates from throughout Vermont convened to ratify the United States Constitution and pave the way for Vermont's entry into the Union as the 14th state. The marker also notes that here were offered up prayers by those returned victorious from the capture of Fort Ticonderoga, and the battles of Bennington and Saratoga. Walk south to the next small green and another monument states that, nearby, the famed abolitionist William Lloyd Garrison edited his antislavery newspaper, *The Journal of the Times*, which agitated for abolition before the Civil War.

BENNINGTON CENTRE CEMETERY

Behind and beside the Old First Church is the Bennington Centre Cemetery, established in 1762, the oldest burying ground in Vermont. Filled with stones that bear unique examples of the American folk art of gravestone carvings, those with angel-like depictions date from the late 1700s, while many from the early 1800s have willow tree and urn motifs. Here are buried five Vermont governors and many important personages of early Vermont. Take note of the large stone monument that bears the inscription: AROUND THIS STONE LIE BURIED MANY PATRIOTS WHO FELL IN THE BATTLE OF BENNINGTON AUGUST 16, 1777 . . . HERE ALSO REST BRITISH SOLDIERS, HESSIANS, WHO DIED FROM WOUNDS AFTER THE BATTLE. AS CAPTIVES THEY WERE CONFINED IN THE FIRST MEETING HOUSE BUILT IN VERMONT, WHICH STOOD IN THE GREEN WEST OF THIS BURYING GROUND. Before leaving the cemetery, wander among its old stones and see many graves of other men who fought in the Revolution. Also walk directly down behind the church to the grave of the poet Robert Frost whose epitaph reads, I HAD A LOVER'S QUARREL WITH THE WORLD. After leaving the cemetery, walk north to the street corner where a marker notes the location of Ethan Allen's Bennington home from 1769–75.

Directions
Drive north along Old Bennington's Monument Street and note on the right the statue of a prowling panther marking the location of the

legendary Catamount Tavern, where Allen and his Green Mountain Boys once gathered to raise the flowing bowl and plan their mischief and exploits. At the end of the street is the great green circle upon which stands the 306-foot-high Bennington Battle Monument.

BENNINGTON BATTLE MONUMENT

The Bennington Monument is open mid-April through October 31, 9–5. Admission fee.

The heroic marble statue of Seth Warner stands directly in front of the mighty obelisk. Circle the monument and on the far side see the new statue of John Stark, sword in hand. Park by the Visitors Center and note the marker by its entrance near the site of the storehouse said to have been one of the objectives of the ill-fated British expedition toward Bennington. An elevator takes visitors more than 200 feet to the monument's observation deck that offers fine views of southwestern Vermont and neighboring New York and Massachusetts. Note that John Burgoyne's cooking kettle, seized at Saratoga, is suspended within the monument's entryway. The monument was dedicated in 1891 with great ceremony, including a speech by President Benjamin Harrison. Among those listening was a Vermont lad named Calvin Coolidge.

Directions
From the monument, return down Old Bennington's Monument Street, turn left on VT 9, and just down the hill on the right is the Bennington Museum.

BENNINGTON MUSEUM

The museum houses important collections of American glassware, paintings, furniture, Bennington pottery, the largest collection of the art and personal memorabilia of Grandma Moses, and other items of

historic and artistic interest. By the museum entrance is a statue of Abraham Lincoln and a monument to the men of Bennington who served in
the Civil War. Of particular interest is a room devoted to the Battle of Bennington. The Lenox
Williams painting *Prisoners Taken in the Battle of
Bennington* depicts the victorious Americans
herding their prisoners into Old Bennington and dominates the room.
Also on display is one of the cannon captured by the Americans at
Bennington, a British drum seized on the battlefield, and a sword surrendered by a Hessian soldier.

The Bennington Museum is open daily, 9–5; closed only on Thanksgiving and from December 23 through January 1. Admission fee.

Directions

From the museum, you may retrace the way back to Schuylerville via
the Bennington Battlefield by taking VT 9 to the center of Bennington,
turning left on VT 7 North, then left turn onto VT 67A. But a pleasant
option is to visit Hildene, the home of Abraham Lincoln's oldest son,
Robert Todd Lincoln, near the village of Manchester, by taking VT 7A
north. The way leads 20 miles north along the Valley of Vermont, between the Green Mountains and the Taconic Mountains, following in
reverse Seth Warner's march from Manchester to fight at Bennington.
You will pass one of the homes of Robert Frost, a place where Ethan
Allen once lived, and through the village of Arlington the painter
Norman Rockwell called home. Stay on VT 7A until the highest of all
the Taconics, Equinox Mountain, looms on the left. At the southern
edge of Manchester Village look for the sign for Hildene on the right.
A long, shaded drive leads to the mansion.

HILDENE

Abraham Lincoln's oldest son Robert Todd Lincoln built a summer
home, Hildene, atop a scenic ridge just south of Manchester. Young
Lincoln, who was present at the death of his father in 1865, had visited Manchester during the Civil War with his mother, Mary Todd

Lincoln. Having attended Harvard, Robert became a successful lawyer like his father. Appointed secretary of war by President Garfield, he also served as minister to Great Britain under President Benjamin Harrison, and later became chairman of the board and president of the Pullman Company. In 1902, at the height of his career, he built Hildene, making it his warmer months' home until his death there in 1926. One of New England's loveliest homes, with formal gardens, Hildene commands grand views of the Valley of Vermont. The estate is lovingly maintained by the Friends of Hildene.

Upon graduation from Harvard in 1864, Robert Lincoln informed his parents that he intended to join the Union armies. President Lincoln had him assigned to Ulysses Grant's staff. Consequently, Lincoln was present at Grant's headquarters during the last weeks of the war and was at Appomattox Court House when Lee surrendered to Grant. Hildene has opened a Civil War exhibit on the mansion's second floor, which not only interprets Robert Lincoln's brief military service, but honors the local Manchester infantry company that sustained heavy casualties, particularly at the Battle of Savage Station in 1862. Among Hildene's treasures are a top hat owned by President Lincoln and an oval mirror into which, according to Robert Lincoln, the president looked before leaving for Ford's Theatre the night of his assassination.

Directions

From Hildene, return south 7 miles along VT 7A, and in Arlington turn right, or west, on VT 313. Proceeding along Batten Kill Valley, one is struck by the sheer beauty of the country and the fertility of its farmlands. Follow VT/NY 313 into NY 372 at Cambridge, and you have rejoined the way you took from Schuylerville to Bennington. At Greenwich, take NY 29 across the Hudson into Schuylerville. Turn north of US 4, and less than a mile along glance up to the left at the brick Marshall House, a survivor of the last siege of the Saratoga campaign. In its basement the Baroness von Riedesel took refuge from American shelling. Half a mile beyond, see a sign on the left for Stark's Knob. Pull over.

STARK'S KNOB

Americans under John Stark, the victor at Bennington, took position here blocking the British retreat. Burgoyne's last chance was gone. A historic marker notes Stark's position, and behind it is one of the many markers along Henry Knox's route. Drive a short way up the road that branches off here and come to a small park on the right. Walk into the park and come to an old quarry where the ancient lava rock of Stark's Knob is exposed. Interpretive signs explain its geology.

Directions
Return to US 4 and continue north, soon crossing the Hudson near where Burgoyne's army crossed. Continue north on US 4, and in 2 miles turn left at another Knox monument and by the sign LOCK SIX. Cross the Champlain Canal on a narrow bridge and drive into the beautiful little village of Fort Miller.

FORT MILLER

Across the Hudson from the village stood Fort Miller, a French and Indian War bastion now long vanished. The fort protected "The Little Carry," a portage around the Hudson River rapids at this site.

Directions
Return to US 4 and a mile north, on the right, see a sign for the Duer House. Pull over.

DUER HOUSE

Burgoyne made his headquarters at the Duer House for nearly a month as he waited for supplies. It was likely here that he enthusiastically greeted what was left of Baum and Breymann's forces that straggled back after the debacle at Bennington. Drive up the side road here a 0.25 mile and a marker identifies the site of the house. Nothing remains of the elegant home that some of Burgoyne's men likened to a castle. Burgoyne's army camped in the fields surrounding the site.

Directions

Proceed north on US 4 for 5 miles and on the left see a marker on the site of Jane McCrea's first burial. Pull over.

Chapter Four

Fort Edward

JANE McCREA MARKER

Approaching Fort Edward, the name Jane McCrea becomes important. Jane, about 24 years old in 1777, was engaged to a Tory officer, David Jones, and she chose to remain in the Fort Edward area despite the approach of hostilities. She took up residence with a local lady, Mrs. Sara McNeil, a cousin of Gen. Simon Fraser. On the approach of a war party roving in advance of Burgoyne's main force, the two women took refuge in the McNeil house. But they were seized and taken by the Indians toward Burgoyne's camp. Apparently, along the way, an argument developed concerning the younger captive. One version of the story holds that one of the Indians became enraged and shot and scalped her. When the bloody trophy was brought to Burgoyne's camp, the hair was recognized by her fiancé. Burgoyne attempted to have the guilty party shot, but was immediately told that if the execution took place, all Indians would desert his army. Burgoyne was forced to let the killer, or killers, go, and that action was seen as proof that the British commander was condoning Indian terrorism against white settlers. Word of Jane McCrea's death spread rapidly through the countryside, rallying opposition to Burgoyne.

Directions

Proceed north on US 4 and on entering Fort Edward, just after crossing the Champlain Canal, look for a stately colonial house, with a marker in front, set back from the road on the left. Pull into the parking lot.

OLD FORT HOUSE MUSEUM

Built as a private residence in 1772 by Patrick Smyth, the house is one of the oldest frame buildings in upstate New York and is the centerpiece of a 3-acre historic campus. The main house, also called the Red House, constructed with timbers from Fort Edward, is literally filled with history—both artifacts and lore. Used briefly as headquarters by Gen. Philip Schuyler in 1777, the house was taken over by the British as the Americans retreated south. Burgoyne wrote in his orderly book, "The headquarters will be at the Red House near Fort Edward, covered by the Riedesel Dragoons, who will encamp on the plain." Also, for a time, Baroness von Riedesel moved in with her husband and children. "We very happily passed three weeks together," she wrote. "The country around us was beautiful, and we were in the midst of the encampment of the British and German troops. We had for our lodgings a dwelling called the Red House . . . When the weather was fine we dined under the trees, and if not, in the barn." George Washington, on his 1783 tour, was at the house both going north and returning south. Also, Benjamin Franklin stopped by on his 1776 trip to inspect the northern army in Canada. A guide at the house noted that the dining room hosted both Washington and Franklin for dinner. The pavilion building behind the main house exhibits a fine model of Fort Edward.

The museum is open daily June through August, and weekends, September 1 through mid-October, 1–5. Admission fee.

Directions

Leaving the house, go north on US 4 and quickly turn right on State Street.

STATE STREET BURYING GROUND

In the State Street Burying Ground, where weathered stones stand in the shade of old maples, Jane McCrea was buried for the second time, and Duncan Campbell, dead of wounds suffered at Ticonderoga, was buried for the first time.

Directions

Return to US 4 via State Street, go just a short distance north, and make a sharp left just before the Anvil Inn onto Montgomery Street. Then turn quickly left onto Fort Street and at the end is a tiny park on the banks of the Hudson with picnic table and bench. Park here. It is hard to believe that you are now adjacent to one of the largest forts ever built in North America.

FORT EDWARD

The village of Fort Edward is a pleasant, tree-shaded town like many along the upper Hudson. Here, where the river makes a great swing to the west, countless generations of Native peoples used the Great Carrying Place at this site, the longest of three portages on the water route between the sea and the St. Lawrence. A road led from here to Lake George. Beneath this part of the modern village of Fort Edward lie the foundations of a massive British fort. Walk the nearby Old Fort, Moon, and Edward streets, and note the uneven ground of the lawns and backyards. Excavations undertaken since 1996 have briefly exposed many parts of the fort. Here stood the ramparts, barracks, and sally ports of old Fort Edward, once the front line of British defense in the Hudson Valley. A sign stands in the shallow depression that was once a 60-foot-wide moat. In this quiet setting the imagination is sorely tested, and it is difficult to conjure up the thousands of soldiers who came here to do battle during the French and Indian War and, later, during the Revolution. The 18th-century fort was formidable, its double thick, 10-foot-

Fort Edward Moat

high log walls filled with earth. Sentries watched from outworks, including blockhouses. Where soldiers once drilled, homeowners now march behind lawnmowers.

The first fortification at the Great Carrying Place, called Fort Nicholson was built in 1709, and manned by 450 soldiers. In 1731, John Henry Lydius built a trading post on the site of the old and abandoned fort. With the outbreak of the French and Indian War, British General William Johnson ordered construction of two forts—one at the southern end of Lake George and one on the Hudson. Capt. William Eyre, noted engineer of the British army, designed both forts and he described Fort Edward in a letter written in September 1755: "I have built a fort at the Carrying Place which will contain 300 men, it is in the form of a square with three bastions and takes in Col Lydius's house, this work is palisaded quite round, which is its chief security from a surprise." Fort Edward was built on the east bank of the Hudson, with the river serving as a moat on the west side. The place contained two large barracks, shops, and a powder magazine, with cannon mounted on the battlements. Eyre also ordered a huge blockhouse, the Royal Blockhouse, built on a knoll overlooking the river's west shore. Ninety feet per side, it was one of the largest blockhouses ever built in North America.

As warfare intensified, soldiers went forth from Fort Edward who suffered the disaster at Fort William Henry in August 1757. The terrified survivors of the massacre wandered back, to be greeted by the garrison that had never gone to their rescue. After that British military debacle, the fort was strengthened, its walls heightened. In 1758, Maj. Gen. James Abercromby assembled his 16,000-man army at Fort Edward, the encampment spreading far and wide over the surrounding river plain and onto the adjacent mile-long island. From Fort Edward, Abercromby and Lord Howe moved north against Montcalm at Fort Carillon. The next year, Jeffery Amherst arrived at Fort Edward to again bring the fight to the French. A calm, methodical man, Amherst made sure his troops were well fed and the fort's ovens produced 2,000 loaves of bread each day. Also, a brewery made barrels of spruce beer to counter scurvy, the greatest killer of troops after smallpox.

On June 17, 1759, under a flag of truce—red, instead of the customary white of the French national flag—a French major and four men appeared at Fort Edward's gate. The parley was ostensibly to negotiate an exchange of prisoners, but Amherst rightly suspected the true intent was to determine his strength. The visitors were allowed a good look at the huge army before returning north. The information obtained was likely a factor in the French commander's decision to blow up and abandon Fort Carillon as Amherst's mighty army drew near.

When the French military was forced out of North America after the fall of Québec in 1760, there no longer was a need for a large force at Fort Edward and the British evacuated the site in 1766. The fort was abandoned for 10 years and fell into disrepair until the American capture of Fort Ticonderoga when it was again garrisoned. In 1777, when John Burgoyne moved south, Philip Schuyler briefly made his headquarters at the dilapidated fortress. When Burgoyne arrived, he set up headquarters in the nearby Smyth house. After the defeat of Burgoyne at Saratoga, the British returned in 1780 and the fort was occupied by a small detachment until 1783, when it was again abandoned. As a village grew up in the area, fort buildings were dismantled for building materials. No battle was ever fought at the great fort, though it did play a major role in the military history of the Champlain Corridor.

Directions

Return to US 4 and go a short distance north to the stoplight. Turn left and cross the bridge. On reaching the far side, between the first and second bridges, you have arrived on Rogers Island. Turn left into the Visitors Center.

ROGERS ISLAND

When you walk upon Rogers Island, you walk where many ranger companies camped and prepared to fight, including men under the legendary Robert Rogers. From here, Rogers led his green-coated Colonials on raids and scouting missions against the French, sifting through the virgin forests and rugged hills and mountains of the dangerous territory that

Rogers Island

Archaeologist and author David Starbuck described the island in his book *Rangers and Redcoats on the Hudson*:

> Fort Edward was the staging area for Abercromby's Army in 1758 before they departed to attack the French breastworks at Fort Carillon (Ticonderoga). After that battle, the wounded provincial troops then returned to the hospitals on Rogers Island that had been set up for their treatment. During this period, British soldiers lived within massive barracks buildings on Rogers Island and within the fort, each perhaps as much as three hundred feet long, whereas provincial soldiers, rangers, and some officers lived in rows of small huts, houses, or tents. Historical records indicate that other structures and features on Rogers Island included a large or "Great Blockhouse" in the center of the island (this was later turned into a hospital), a large storehouse for provisions, a smallpox hospital at the south end of the island, a sawpit, and small privies or "necessary houses" located along both riverbanks. Extensive gardens were planted, both on the island and on the east bank of the Hudson River, that provided fresh vegetables for the soldiers.

separated French from British forces. Rogers Island, a mile long, lies in the Hudson opposite the site of Fort Edward, stretching well to the north and south of the fort. As the British built and garrisoned Fort Edward, they brought large armies there; during the warmer months thousands of troops camped on the nearby flat and sandy island.

The Rogers Island Visitors Center is open daily, June through August, Monday through Saturday, 10–4 and Sunday 1–4. Closed Monday and Tuesday, September through May.

ROGERS ISLAND VISITORS CENTER

Opened in the summer of 2001 in an old Mobil Oil Company building, the facility contains exhibits on prehistoric times and on the

---

Starbuck, who has led extensive archaeological digs on Rogers Island, also notes that the most famous officer ever to die in the Rogers Island hospital was Major Duncan Campbell of the 42nd Highland Regiment, the man who, Robert Lewis Stevenson wrote, had his death before the walls of Ticonderoga foretold in the Scottish Highlands.

But the name Rogers dominates the island's history, and it was on the island that Rogers wrote down his famed rules for frontier fighting. They included an insistence that men on the march act as they would in sneaking up on a deer, that muskets be clean at all times, that no unnecessary chances be taken, and that marchers always be far apart when in single file. Also, a party of men should never return the way they came, to prevent ambush, and if pursued, should form a circle and set up their own ambush. From Rogers Island, his Rangers scouted the French forts at Crown Point and Ticonderoga. From here they went forth on the expedition that resulted in the Battle on Shoe Shoes near Ticonderoga and the clash at Point au Fer on the northern lake.

Open 10–4, Monday through Saturday, June 1 to September 1, and 1–4, Sunday, Labor Day to May 30; 10–4, Wednesday through Saturday, and 1–4, Sunday. Free admission.

military history of the 18th century. Many of the artifacts on display were dug up under Starbuck's supervision at the archaeology field school that he heads each summer at various sites in Fort Edward. The center shows a variety of videos, including a Learning Channel production on Rogers Island featuring Starbuck's explorations. While most of the island is private property and closed to visitors, it is the center's hope that the entire island will soon become state property and all, or most of it, will be open to the public.

Directions

From the Visitors Center, turn right on NY 197 and at the stoplight in Fort Edward, turn left, or north. As you go uphill toward the Fort Edward High School, look for a monument (it stands between two houses), on the spot where Jane McCrea was killed. Proceed north on US 4 until you see a large burying ground, Union Cemetery, on the right. Just through the gate, within an iron fence, are the graves of Duncan Campbell and Jane McCrea.

UNION CEMETERY

Duncan Campbell and Jane McCrea finally came to permanent rest, side by side, in this large, well-kept cemetery. This was Campbell's second resting place, having been moved from the graveyard near Fort Edward. McCrea was exhumed from this, her third grave, in 2003. Only a partial skeleton was found, apparently confirming rumors that some of her bones were pirated at the time of her third burial. Another skeleton found in the grave, that of a larger and older woman, was confirmed through scientific analysis to be that of Sara McNeil. Both women have been returned to their rest here.

Directions

Return south on US 4, and turn right again on NY 197. Pass the Rogers Island Visitors Center, and as you cross the bridge to the west bank of the Hudson, take note of the prominent hill that rises on the right above the road. Its summit is the location of the huge Royal Blockhouse, the largest of Fort Edward's outer works. Follow NY 197 for 4 miles to US 9, turn left and in 1 mile turn onto I-87 north. Take Exit 20, and go north on US 9 into Lake George Village. Look for a sign for the Fort William Henry Conference Center on the right and pull into its parking lot.

Chapter Five

Lake George

LAKE GEORGE VILLAGE

Lake George's European history commenced in 1646 when Father Isaac Jogues, a French Jesuit missionary, brought his religion to the Iroquois and named the water Lac du Saint Sacrement. When he first saw the beautiful body of water, Father Jogues had already experienced Indian enmity when, four years previous, as a missionary to the Hurons, he had been captured by Iroquois and tortured by having a thumb and forefinger chewed to stumps. Rescued by the Dutch, he returned to France to recuperate, still dreaming of his wilderness missionary work. Obtaining a special dispensation from the pope to serve Mass with his mutilated hand, he went back to New France to continue his work among the Indians. Soon back in the wilds, the priest was tomahawked to death, his head impaled on a stake. Nearly three centuries later, the Catholic Church made Father Jogues a saint.

In 1755, when Great Britain determined to oust the French from their possessions, campaigns also were planned to capture Fort Duquesne, Fort Niagara, and Fort Beauséjour in Nova Scotia. Also,

Note: Lake George Village is a highly popular resort community, and traffic is often daunting in the summer months. But its military sites must be seen, and some are located in settings of true beauty.

Statue of Father Jogues at Lake George

William Johnson was to advance down Lake George and Lake Champlain to capture Crown Point. From Fort Edward, under construction, Johnson ordered a road cut to the head of Lac du Saint Sacrement where a new fort was to be built. Johnson named the rising bastion Fort William Henry, honoring the king's grandson. Johnson had with him a friend, Theyanoguin, a Mohawk chief. King Hendrick, as he was called by the English, had long before visited England and had met Queen Anne. By 1755 he was old, but he retained his power and charisma as leader of the Mohawks. Also at Lake George was Col. Ephraim Williams of the Massachusetts militia. A successful lawyer, Williams had already designated funds in his will to establish a college at Williamstown, Massachusetts.

Soon word reached the garrison that French General Jean-Armand Dieskau was moving south from Crown Point to attack Fort Edward. To meet the advance, Johnson, on September 8, ordered out a detachment of 200 Indians led by 75-year-old King Hendrick and 1,000 provincials. Ephraim Williams rode in the lead of what would become famous as the "Early Morning Scout." Dieskau, with a force of only about 800 men had already determined that an attack on Fort Edward was hopeless. So he diverted his attention to Lake George and, learning of the English detachment's approach, lay in ambush south of the unfinished fort. Hendrick and Williams had gone only about 3 miles south along a ravine when shots rang out and, according to Dieskau, the head of the British column doubled up "like a pack of cards." Williams, climbing a slope to the right to rally his men, was shot dead. Old Hendrick's horse was shot from under him, and he was bayoneted through the heart by a French grenadier.

A crude breastwork of logs, stumps, and wagons was hastily erected at the English camp and armed with three cannons. Dieskau followed close on the heels of the detachment he had routed, hoping to follow them into camp. But the British were ready and the ensuing battle, known as the Battle of Lake George, raged for four hours. Johnson was severely wounded and Gen. Phineas Lyman of Connecticut led the defense fighting off repeated attacks. "There seemed to be nothing but thunder and lightening & perpetual pillars of smoke," wrote Thomas Williams, brother of the slain Ephraim. At last, Dieskau ordered a final attack, which the British met with their own assault. In the final desperate fighting, the French were sent north in retreat and Dieskau was wounded and captured. He died of his wounds back in France in 1767.

While that battle raged, some Canadians and Indians who had ambushed the English were busy looting the bodies when they were surprised by reinforcements from Fort Edward. Legend holds that so many were killed that a nearby pond turned red when their bodies were dumped into it; ever since the place has been known as Bloody Pond.

So ended the Battle of Lake George, fought and won by the British. By November, Fort William Henry, with its 30-foot-thick walls, storehouses, powder magazines, and two-story barracks, stood completed on a bluff overlooking Lake George. Meanwhile, to the north on Lake Champlain, the French were themselves building a fort at the place where Dieskau's defeated force had camped—they called it Fort Carillon.

Marquis Louis-Joseph de Montcalm-Gozon de Saint Veran, the bold General Montcalm, was appointed to replace Dieskau as major general of the French army in Canada. He arrived in Canada in 1756 and found that he was under the jurisdiction of suspicious and critical Governor Philippe de Rigaud, marquis de Vaudreuil. In March 1757, Vaudreuil, apparently jealous of Montcalm's reputation, sent a force under the leadership of his brother François-Pierre Rigaud to attack Fort William Henry. Though the French attack failed, they did succeed in weakening the British fort by burning outbuildings and many boats.

Montcalm now set about assembling a large army at Carillon that moved south on August 1 with some 8,000 men, including 1,800 Indians. Two-thirds of the force came south on Lake George in a great flotilla, while the rest moved through the forests on the lake's west side. By dawn on August 3 they all faced Fort William Henry, and its 2,300-man garrison. The French set about digging siege trenches as cannon were brought ashore. Meanwhile, Indians blocked the British route of escape and support to Fort Edward.

The afternoon of August 3, Montcalm sent a message to Colonel George Monro, the British commander, asking him to surrender. "I have it yet in my power to restrain the savages, and to oblige them to observe a capitulation, as none of them have as yet been killed," Montcalm wrote. Monro replied that there would be no surrender, and soon the fort was under heavy fire, as was the fortified camp located on high ground to the east. Meanwhile, to the south at Fort Edward, General Daniel Webb in command there refused to send help.

The siege lasted until August 9, with the French moving their lines, and guns, ever closer. On August 7 another surrender demand was taken to the battered fort and that, too, was rejected. But two days later Monro raised a white flag over his weakened walls. Under the terms agreed to, a guard of French regulars was to escort captives safely to Fort Edward. Montcalm conferred with the Indian chiefs asking them to control their warriors and to let the British keep their possessions. Still, the ensuing two days became ones of horror.

When the English emerged from the fort, the Indians rushed in and killed the sick and wounded. Terrified, the defeated English spent the night as prisoners in their nearby fortified camp, then were ordered to walk south the next morning. As the column moved toward, or into, the ravine through which the military road led south to Fort Edward, the captives were set upon by Indians. Women, children, and unarmed soldiers were taken or, if they resisted, killed indiscriminately. Amid it all, the British prevailed on the French to stop the slaughter, only to be told to escape as best they could. Estimates of the killed vary from 180 to more than 300. Survivors fled into the woods and made their way to Fort Edward. Francis Parkman wrote that back at William Henry, "The barracks were torn down, and the huge pine logs of the rampart thrown into a heap. The dead bodies that filled the casemates were added to the mass, and fire was set to the whole. The mighty funeral pyre blazed all night."

In the summer of 1758, General Abercromby's army massed near Fort William Henry's blackened ruins for its doomed assault on Carillon. A few days later the army straggled back, having sustained some 2,000 casualties. In 1759, Amherst brought his army to the ruined fort, then moved north to capture Carillon. But before departing, he ordered construction of a new fort overlooking Lake George. His chief engineer, James Montresor, chose the site of William Henry's fortified camp. Never completed, the fort had walls 14 feet thick, built of stone. Some barracks were completed and a dozen cannon mounted. For 16 quiet years, Fort George stood by peaceful waters. Then when Ticonderoga was captured in 1775, a detachment of Green Mountain Boys seized it without incident. In July, Philip Schuyler arrived and the Americans built a hospital near the fort, to which the sick and wounded came from the failed Canadian campaign. In 1776, Benjamin Franklin inspected Fort George on his way to Canada, finding it in a ruinous state.

In 1777, with Burgoyne's advance, General Schuyler ordered Fort George destroyed. The British reported finding at the head of the lake "a small square fort faced with masonry . . . The Rebels . . . blew up the Magazine on the side next the water which demolished the face." They also found a hospital building "of great dimensions." Later that year, as Burgoyne moved south, the Americans reclaimed Fort George. The British reoccupied the place in 1780, but were gone by 1783 when George Washington visited. Jefferson and Madison came in 1791 and Jefferson wrote: "Lake George is without comparison the most beautiful water I ever saw; formed by contours of the mountains . . . finely interspersed with islands, its water limpid as crystal."

FORT WILLIAM HENRY

Touring the Fort

Open May 1 through October 31, daily, 9–6. Call 518-668-5471 for more information. Admission fee.

From the lot where you have already parked, a log structure is visible on the south side where human skeletons found at Fort William Henry were once displayed; but they have long been removed and some were reburied on Memorial Day in 1993. Excavations suggest that the fort parking lot covers a military cemetery with more than 3,000 graves.

Fort William Henry, which stood for just two years, became one of the world's most famous forts due to the publication, in the 19th century, of Cooper's novel *The Last of the Mohicans*, which told the story of the massacre. Today the grim, dark-walled fort hunkers down on its bluff facing Lake George, a sinister contrast to summer-happy vacationers lolling on Million Dollar Beach. The structure is a faithful, 1950s replica of the original structure that was burned in 1757. A monument near the fort's entrance was erected by the Royal Sussex Regiment Association to the memory of the officers and men of the 35th Regiment of Foot, their wives and children, who were victims of the siege and massacre. On approaching the fort's entryway, notice the moat. The fort is entered through its gift shop and display area. Beyond is the parade ground where the 400 soldiers who once manned the place assembled. Barracks rise, faithful reconstructions of the original structures. The fort well, dug by Rogers' Rangers in 1756, is preserved and the fort offers an intriguing display of thousands of coins and assorted items, tossed in by recent visitors, and pulled up from its depths by archaeologist Starbuck. Stairs descend to the fort's lower levels, to the dungeon and casemates where some of the fort's sick and wounded were slain in 1757. From the fort's walls, looking north down beautiful Lake George, one can ponder having been a British soldier witnessing the approach of the vast French flotilla bringing the army that laid siege to the fort. From the east wall, the view is across a parkland, which was a swamp at the time of the French and Indian War, to the location of the fortified camp on the pine ridge beyond.

Directions

From the Fort William Henry parking lot, you may wish to walk north along Canada Street (US 9) about 0.25 mile to Shepard Park. Proceed to the waterfront and you'll be in the area where Montcalm landed. If you walk just past the park, you'll come to the old court house, which is now a museum.

LAKE GEORGE
HISTORICAL ASSOCIATION MUSEUM

The museum is located in the 1845 Lake George Court House, beautifully preserved with its tin walls and ceilings. The old jail cells in the

Open late May through June, Saturday and Sunday, 11–4; July and August, Friday, Saturday and Tuesday; 11–4; September, Friday, Saturday, and Sunday, 11–4; the first two weeks in October. Free, though donations are encouraged.

basement are open to visitors. The museum also displays an intricate model of a church, made of cigar boxes, the work of a condemned prisoner, who sold his creation to pay for a lawyer. His conviction was reversed. But more in keeping with military history, the museum has a small but impressive display of wartime artifacts found in and around Lake George, and has an electronic display panel that tells the story of various important local historic sites.

Directions

Return down Canada Street and turn left on Beach Street and you will come to the docks from which Lake George cruise boats operate.

LAKE GEORGE CRUISES

Trips vary from full-day trips the length of the 32-mile lake, to one-hour trips, to lunch, dinner, and moonlight cruises. Prices vary.

The cruise boats offer narrations on the lake's history and points of interest. Historic sites noted along the way include Diamond Island, where Burgoyne located a supply base, Sabbathday Point, where Indians sprung a bloody ambush on British troops just prior to the siege of Fort William Henry, and Rogers Rock, near the lake's north end, where it is said Rogers narrowly escaped capture.

Directions

Return to the Fort William Henry parking lot, drive north on Canada Street, and quickly turn right on Beach Road. Proceed along the beach and turn right onto Old Fort George Road. You soon come to a sign on the left for the Lake George Battlefield Park, Campground, and Picnic Area. Turn in here. A tour road leads through the park.

LAKE GEORGE BATTLEFIELD PARK

Touring Lake George Battlefield Park

The park is located on land that once was encompassed by the fortified camps of William Johnson's army and of a part of the British army
that came under siege with the Fort William Henry garrison. There is
much history to discover here. On entering the
park, you are in the area that would have been
under fire during the French attack on Johnson's
army in 1755 at the Battle of Lake George. Following the tour road, the stone mass of Fort
George suddenly rises ahead, the only one of its bastions that was ever
completed and still survives, thanks to a 20th-century reconstruction.
Nearby mounds of earth are likely remains of other portions of the unfinished fort. The location of the large American smallpox hospital at
Fort George is unknown. Continue on past the fort and look to the
right, the east. The land drops away at this edge of the park and atop
the drop-off look for remnants of the fortifications of the 1757 fortified camp, now just low rises of earth. Continue on to the parking area
that overlooks the lake and make a mental note that when you reach
Fort Ticonderoga, you will again see this view in the famous painting
by Thomas Davies.

> Open early May through
> Labor Day. Call 518-668-
> 3352 for more informa-
> tion. Admission fee.

By the parking lot is an impressive statue of King Hendrick and
William Johnson talking over strategy for the Early Morning Scout.
Stand with your back to the Johnson/Hendrick statue and look across
the Fort George Road at the impressive statue of Father Jogues. The
priest's robes flow behind as he holds a cross, while his mutilated hand
is raised in benediction. His eyes are fixed on the lake he named.

Walk about the park and look for disturbances in the earth and
remnants of stone foundations. All are part of the military history of
the place. David Starbuck found the remains of soldier huts and barracks everywhere when he dug here in 2000 and 2001. In this area the
terrified garrison of Fort William Henry was assembled to be marched
south toward Fort Edward.

Directions
From the Lake George Battlefield Park, turn left on Fort George Road.

MILITARY ROAD

The Fort George Road follows the old military road and in taking it south from the area of the Fortified Camp, you will be on the route taken by the doomed captives as they started their trek south toward Fort Edward. No one seems absolutely certain where the massacre began, but some historians feel it commenced in the area where the Fort George Road meets busy and commercial US 9. Also in this area, the French launched their attacks against the British camp in 1755. A bike path runs south along an old railroad bed from the battlefield park; if you follow it you'll be on, or very close to, the old military road. Certainly it was a route of terror on that fateful morning in 1757. Moving south along US 9 from Lake George Village, there are several opportunities to park and walk along a portion of the bike path. Park at the corner of US 9 and Bloody Pond Road and go south. About a half-mile of biking or walking will bring you to the area of Bloody Pond.

Directions
Continue driving south on US 9 and on the west side of the road, opposite the King Hendrick Motel, look for a sign identifying Ephraim Williams's Grave. Pull over carefully, for there is little room for parking and traffic is often heavy.

EARLY MORNING SCOUT SITE

Behind the Williams sign, a stone marks the resting place of the founder of Williams College. Carefully cross the heavily traveled road and just north of the Hendrick Motel, you will see a path descend behind the guardrail. Follow it into the famed ravine where the Early

Morning Scout was ambushed. A monument stands atop the large boulder where Williams was killed. Walk deeper into the ravine. Though the traffic noise from US 9 can be heard, you may find it easy to imagine how an ambush took place there, amid the tall trees, on the morning of the Battle of Lake George. Also through this ravine, in this area, came terrified captives from Fort William Henry trying to escape the 1757 massacre.

Directions

Return to your car, carefully crossing the busy road, then take US 9 south to its junction with NY 149 amid a busy shopping area. Turn east on NY 149 and drive some 12 miles until reaching the village of Fort Ann. Turn left (north) onto US 4.

Chapter Six

Fort Ann and Whitehall

FORT ANN

The Fort Ann bank building, on the northern edge of the village, is a dark, square, wooden blockhouse, an odd sight in a small peaceful town. A real blockhouse once stood here, amid an untamed and dangerous wilderness. Certainly, things were anything but peaceful when Col. Francis Nicholson came here to build a fort in 1709. After cutting a road from Albany to Wood Creek, Nicholson's 1,600 men built a palisaded blockhouse, intending to move on to invade Québec. The offensive failed, though Nicholson returned in 1711, this time to burn the fort. The structure's charred remains were still visible in 1749 when the Swedish naturalist Peter Kalm visited the area.

One of the French and Indian War's famous escape stories occurred in this area in 1758 as Robert Rogers, Israel Putnam, and a group of rangers walked into an ambush near Fort Ann's clearing. Putnam was dragged captive into the woods while Rogers and the rest fled. Putnam was tied to a tree and his Indian captors, for a time, threw hatchets toward his head, seeing how close they could come. A Canadian soldier then pushed a musket against Putnam's chest and pulled the trigger, but the gun misfired. That night Putnam was stripped and tied to a tree, about which dry branches were piled. But when ignited, a sudden rain doused the fire. More wood was gathered and a new fire started, but a French soldier kicked away the burning sticks. Putnam survived, was interrogated by Montcalm, and later exchanged.

Fort Ann was a defensive position, again a palisaded blockhouse, during the Revolution. Just north of Fort Ann, Burgoyne's advance troops met stiff resistance from Philip Schuyler's men guarding the American rear. The fight happened on July 8, 1777, as the American forces who had departed Fort Ticonderoga and Mount Independence via Lake Champlain and Skenesborough turned on their British pursuers who were led by Lt. Col. John Hill. The result was a vicious little battle that sent the British retreating to Skenesborough. Richard Ketchum wrote in his book *Saratoga*: "'As at Hubbardton, anything resembling a battle formation was out of the question, and visibility was virtually nil because of the thick trees and craggy ground. The rebels, slanting through the trees, crossed Wood Creek, turned Hill's left, and worked their way behind him; he couldn't see them but could tell from their voices that he would soon be surrounded, so he ordered his men to withdraw up the precipitous slope to their rear—a critical move as Burgoyne later described it (taking care that it should not sound like a retreat), that was executed 'with the utmost steadiness and bravery.'" The two-hour battle resulted in significant casualties and a British retreat. Burgoyne's campaign had been dealt its second telling blow, the first having occurred at Hubbardton. Surely Burgoyne should have rushed reinforcements to Fort Ann to hold the ground since his second advance there would be a much longer and more difficult matter.

Directions
Proceed north from the village of Fort Ann on US 4 and pass through a swampy area. North of the swamp a ridge rises to the left of the highway; and it's likely that the British withdrew up its slope in order to face the American attack. Continue north on US 4.

BURGOYNE ROUTE

The drive north on US 4 closely follows Burgoyne's 1777 march from Skenesborough, or Whitehall, to Fort Ann. The Champlain Canal, which also parallels the road, approximately follows old Wood Creek. While the land today seems rather even and open, look closely at the wayside, especially in the first few miles. The swamps and little streams that delayed the British march are everywhere. Philip Schuyler detached Herrick's Rangers to slow Burgoyne, and they dammed watercourses, destroyed bridges, and felled trees.

Directions
Proceed north on US 4 and entering the village of Whitehall, bear right to continue on US 4 at the traffic light, then turn quick left after crossing the bridge and proceed to the Skenesborough Museum.

WHITEHALL

Whitehall, at the southern tip of Lake Champlain, has the look and feel of a sleepy 19th-century working-class town. But don't be deceived, for history touched this small town with a rather heavy hand, and Whitehall becomes ever more aware of, and caring for, its history. Indeed, the town claims title to being "The Birthplace of the United States Navy" and the evidence presented is convincing. Today, located at the confluence of east–west US 4 and north–south NY 22, in past years this was the point where travelers, foregoing Lake George, began the land journey from the southern tip of Lake Champlain to the Hudson River at Fort Edward.

Founded by Philip Skene in 1759 as the colonial town of Skenesborough, Whitehall was one of the first permanent settlements on Lake Champlain. When Skene arrived, a fort had already been built on the highest point in what is now the downtown area, where the Presbyterian Church stands. Skene, born of a well-placed Scottish family who lived in London, was loyalist to the core and remained faithful to the crown throughout the American Revolution, at a high personal cost.

On May 9, 1775, a small band of American rebels under Samuel Herrick arrived at Whitehall and took possession of the settlement. There in the harbor was the *Katherine*, a trading schooner owned by

Skene. Local historians claim it became the first ship of the U.S. Navy when it was taken to Crown Point, armed, and renamed *Liberty*, then employed by Benedict Arnold to capture at Saint Jean the British ship renamed the *Enterprise*. More important, in the summer of 1776, construction began on the lakeshore at Skenesborough of a fleet of American vessels. It being well known to the Americans that a British force was massing to the north, construction was hastened, first supervised by Philip Schuyler, then by Benedict Arnold. High wages were advertised and workers from the shipyards of Rhode Island, Connecticut, Massachusetts, New York, New Jersey, and Philadelphia arrived, eventually constituting a workforce of 500. The product of its labor was the small fleet that set out north on August 24 and included the schooners *Enterprise, Royal Savage, Revenge*, and *Liberty*, and the gondolas *New Haven, Boston, Providence, Spitfire, Philadelphia*, and *Connecticut*. Built with green wood, the gondolas and schooners were manned mainly by untrained sailors and were destined to do battle with British ships near Valcour Island. Due in part to what happened at Skenesborough, it was 1777 before the king's army was able to get here, and by then the strong resistance was building that would culminate at Saratoga.

The summer of 1777, warring armies came to Whitehall with the American retreat from Fort Ticonderoga and Mount Independence. A long procession of boats heavily laden with disabled American soldiers and their provisions limped to the waterfront on July 8, 1777, with the British close behind. The Americans fled south into the woods with the shouts of their pursuers audible. John Burgoyne, foregoing the Lake George route south, had chosen to pursue the Americans by land, via Skenesborough and Fort Ann. At Whitehall, he seems to have enjoyed a visit of many days duration as the guest of Philip Skene, taking up residence with his mistress, known to the troops as "Mrs. Commisary," in Skene's large stone house. As he rested, his men set off into the swamps and wilds to the south, to cut their way to Fort Ann and beyond.

After the Revolution, Whitehall became a busy boat-building and shipping center. Then, as the War of 1812 began, the town became a supply base for American forces on Champlain. To Whitehall, after his stunning victory over at Plattsburgh in 1814, came Thomas Macdonough with his battered but victorious fleet and captured British vessels. After the war, the ships were moved to the mouth of East Bay just north of Whitehall, where they eventually settled to the bottom and remain, the haunt of underwater archaeologists. Some Whitehall residents recall skating on East Bay in their childhood, and sitting atop the ships' masts. In 1959, to mark Whitehall's bicentennial, one ship was raised and moved to the side of the Champlain Canal in downtown Whitehall. It rests there today, the 119-foot-long hull of the *Ticonderoga*, which fought with Macdonough at Plattsburgh.

SKENESBOROUGH MUSEUM

For a quick lesson in Whitehall's rich history, visit the Skenesborough Museum on Skenesborough Drive, just off Whitehall's Main Street. Located in the 1917 Champlain Canal Terminal building, the museum presents exhibits on the town's past. Most interesting is a diorama of Whitehall's harbor at the time of the Revolutionary War. Artifacts include a large collection of Native American projectile points, a cannon from the War of 1812, and the keystone from the entrance to Philip Skene's manor house with his initials PKS and the date 1770 inscribed. Certainly John Burgoyne passed beneath that stone many times.

The museum is open daily, 10–4, June 15 to Labor Day, 12–4, Sunday. Open weekends, mid-September through October.

Behind the museum, along the Champlain Canal, rests what is left of the *Ticonderoga*. Also, the tour boat *Carillon* sets forth on Sunday, Monday, and Tuesday, at 1 PM, for a cruise down the lake. On the way you will encounter Fiddler's Elbow, near where it is believed Arnold built his fleet, and Put's Rock, where Israel Putnam ambushed an Indian war party coming up the lake in canoes, killing as many as 300 braves. Put's Rock is on private land and can be seen only from the water.

Touring Whitehall

The best place to see Whitehall is from the cliff that rises on the east side of the canal. From the museum, take Main Street north and quickly turn right onto the Saunders Street Bridge. Turn right into Williams Street and quickly take the first left onto Wilson Avenue. Turn left and then take a quick right onto Cliff Street and follow it to its end, atop the ledge high above town. Be careful, for the streets are narrow and some are steep. On the way up, look for stone houses dating back before the War of 1812. Archaeological excavations by the house from which a long stone foundation extends have identified it as a barracks for American troops during the War of 1812. At the end of Cliff Street is the town's Civil War monument, a massive cannon mounted upon a stone pedestal. From the cannon's base, Whitehall is at your feet, the canal, the downtown, and the lakefront. Be careful, the drop-off is precipitous. Carol Greenough, the town's unofficial historian, on taking visitors to the place, simply waves her hand northward to indicate the general area where Arnold built his boats. Return to, and cross, the Saunders Street Bridge. Turn right on Main Street and by the lock see a historic marker for Whitehall Harbor. Continue down to the marina and find, on your right, in a small park, a marker commemorating the birth of the U. S. Navy. Arnold likely built his fleet some distance north of this point. Turn around and return to US 4.

Directions
From downtown Whitehall, head east on US 4 for Hubbardton Battlefield. Take US 4 for 6 miles to the Vermont border, where it becomes a four-lane road, and continue 7 miles to the Castleton exit. Turn left, or north, on the road to Hubbardton. In a little less than 4 miles you'll come to one of Vermont's more handsome farms, the Ransomvale Farm, in whose fields part of St. Clair's army camped the night of July 6, 1777. Two miles beyond, on the left at the hilltop, is the Hubbardton Battlefield Visitors Center.

Note: Efforts to find the exact location of the old fort at Whitehall have thus far been unsuccessful and some locals believe that reconstruction of NY 22, many years ago, wiped out what remained. Archaeologists have thus far been unable to locate the stone house of Philip Skene that lies somewhere at the base of the hill east of town.

Chapter Seven

The Battle of Hubbardton

HUBBARDTON BATTLEFIELD

To the hills of Hubbardton, south via a rough military road, in early July 1777 came the army of Arthur St. Clair on its retreat from Mount Independence and Fort Ticonderoga. While the

Open late May through mid-October, Wednesday through Sunday, 9:30–5.

main body of the army moved on to Castleton, with some units camping at Ransomvale, St. Clair left a rear guard at the settlement of Hubbardton. Under the overall command of Vermont's Seth Warner—and including Massachusetts militia led by Col. Ebenezer Francis and the 2nd New Hampshire Regiment under another Nathan Hale, the rear guard totaled some 1,200 troops. Warner's men camped on Sucker Brook, leaving sentries along the military road in the notch, or saddle, of Sargent Hill above. Burgoyne had ordered a pursuit by 850 British regulars commanded by Brig.-Gen. Simon Fraser supported by some 200 Germans under Baron von Riedesel. The British force camped briefly the night of July 6 at Lacey's Camp, at the north end of Lake Bomoseen, then resumed its trek into the hills at 3 AM on July 7.

Arriving at Hubbardton, the Americans discovered that a raiding party of British and Indians had just swept through the area and several local citizens had been killed or taken prisoner. Indeed, a Mrs.

NANCY CASSIDY

Annual Revolutionary War living-history encampment to commemorate the anniversary of the Battle of Hubbardton.

Boardman and her two children were found by Warner's men under a bed in the Selleck family's cabin, still in hiding. The cabin's owners, John and Sarah Selleck, had fled the area. Warner met with Francis and Hale in the cabin on the eve of battle.

According to historian John Williams, the first encounter came in the saddle of Sargent Hill, probably just after 5 AM on July 7, between American pickets and the British advance. The big fight erupted along Sucker Brook where the British, with the Germans still well in the rear, encountered a firing line under Seth Warner. British officer Joshua Pell wrote that "the Rebels consisted of near two thousand, and form'd behind the enclosures, which in this Country are compos'd of large Trees, laid one upon the other and made a strong breastwork." British Maj. Robert Grant was killed in the battle's opening minutes. At some point as the battle began, Warner sent a detachment to the north, apparently to alert people living in the area. Among those who took heed was Mary Churchill who, with her husband Samuel, owned about 3,000 Hubbardton acres. Starting out on horseback, Mary's mount was hit by a British bullet. According to legend, upon seeing the assailant, Mrs.

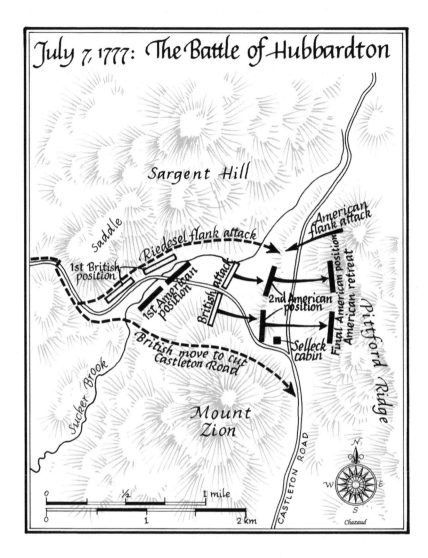

Churchill ran to a startled British soldier and tried to wrest a musket from his hands.

Along Sucker Brook, it must have quickly become apparent to the experienced British soldiers that the Americans were well prepared to put up a stout fight. Warner's men gave ground only grudgingly, moving slowly from the brook to the crest of what is now called Monument Hill. The Americans stood firm there for a time, driving back one British advance, and even counterattacking. But as British pressure increased, Warner withdrew his men toward the Castleton Road, to a position some 200 yards from the hill's crest. After fighting there briefly, the Americans again withdrew to the protection of a farmer's log fence on the east side of the Castleton Road. Joseph Bird, who fought with the Americans, said, "We drove them back twice, cutting them down so fast. We didn't leave (the) log fence or charge them." The American battle line now extended some 800 yards and as the British came on, Nathan Hale ordered his men to attack the left flank of the advancing British. The maneuver caught the British by surprise and was going well until Hale's men were, themselves, caught in the flank. General Fraser, seeing the need for help, had sent word to the approaching German troops under von Riedesel to hurry forward. The Germans came into battle on the British left with flags flying, a brass band blaring, and, some said, singing Lutheran hymns. In Fraser's words, the Germans attacked "in the handsomest manner possible" and the American right began to give way. Warner quickly ordered a retreat. Having discovered that British troops occupied the road south, by which St. Clair's main body had passed, Warner told his men to flee as best they could, to the east over Pittsford Ridge. Sometime late in the fighting, Colonel Francis was killed.

The fight at Hubbardton, long viewed as an American defeat, was finally put in proper perspective more than a half-century ago through the lengthy investigations of Vermont historian John P. Clement, who determined, accurately, that the Americans had waged a successful rear guard action. Losses on both sides were heavy, with more than one fourth of those engaged becoming casualties. Williams put British losses at 50 killed and 134 wounded, with 10 Germans killed and 14 wounded. American losses, Williams said, were 41 killed and 96 wounded, with 234 taken prisoner. The British pursuit of St. Clair was brought to a halt, and St. Clair moved on through Rutland and south to Manchester to fight again. Many Americans who got away over Pittsford Ridge would again battle Burgoyne's troops. The British remained at Hubbardton for several days, burying their dead and treating the wounded. At Hubbardton, the first blow to Burgoyne's ambitious campaign had been dealt.

Touring Hubbardton Battlefield

Edwin Bearss, former National Park Service chief historian and the foremost authority on American battlefields, has said that Hubbardton best retains its setting at the time of battle among all Civil War and Revolutionary War battlefields. It is also one of the loveliest. From the Visitors Center views extend south down the Taconic Range and west toward the southern Adirondacks of New York State. The rock summit of nearby Mount Zion dominates the nearby terrain.

BATTLE MONUMENT

A monument to the Americans who fought at Hubbardton, erected on the spot where the British are said to have buried Colonel Francis, stands by the parking lot. The 1859 white granite shaft is among the oldest Revolutionary War battlefield monuments.

Visitors Center

The Visitors Center electric map provides a fine overview of the battle. A diorama portrays American troops contesting a British attack up Monument Hill. On display are some of the few battle relics that have been found at Hubbardton. Carl Fuller, who grew up in the Fuller house, built long after the battle along Sucker Brook, is now a site interpreter. He says that when walking the fields around the Visitors Center, where intense fighting must have occurred, he occasionally feels presences so intense that he sometimes looks over his shoulder.

MONUMENT HILL TRAIL

From the Visitors Center, a trail loops about the summit of Monument Hill and goes on to the Selleck Cellar Hole. About a half mile in length, the trail is easy walking. It first leads to the crest of Monument Hill, where Americans fought off British attacks for a time from behind log barricades erected along a stone wall. Some of the stones in the wall that now line the crest are probably witnesses to the battle. This area provides an excellent view of Sargent Hill and the gap through which ran the military road used by the Americans and British. Several signs along the trial explain the battle, including one that marks the Americans' second position after their withdrawal from the crest. Then the trail descends to the location of the Selleck home.

SELLECK CELLAR HOLE

The frontier cabin that stood here during the battle most likely did not have a cellar hole. But this is certainly the location of the Selleck home that was used by the Americans as a headquarters and, perhaps, as a hospital by the British after the battle. It was here that the Americans found a frightened frontier family hiding under a bed. Here it is said that Seth Warner met with his commanders, Nathan Hale and the doomed Colonel Francis. Return by path up the hill to the parking lot.

EAST HUBBARDTON CEMETERY

From the parking lot, turn south on Monument Hill Road and turn right on St. John Road just past the Selleck site. Turn right on Frog Pond Road and where it turns sharp left, pull into the road on the right. This leads about 100 yards to the East Hubbardton Cemetery. Walk among the stones and find the graves of John and Sarah Selleck, who returned to their cabin in 1784 after peace had come. On returning, they found and buried many soldier bones. Also find the graves of Samuel and Mary Churchill, she who tried to wrestle a musket from a British regular.

SUCKER BROOK

Return to Frog Pond Road and drive to the old farmhouse of the Fuller Farm on the left, pulling off the road in the driveway. Look across the road and you are looking toward Sucker Brook, which flows through the brushy field behind the barn. The intense fighting at Hubbardton began here. The British advanced down the hill across the brook. The American battle line for a time was formed near where the house now stands. The British deployed and advanced into the fray from the base of the hill to your front. The Americans withdrew to your right and rear up Monument Hill. You may walk into the field behind the barn and down across Sucker Brook. On the far side, if you look closely in the woods, a trace of the military road is visible and can be followed even to the notch of Sargent Hill, after a healthy climb.

MOUNT ZION

From the Fuller Farm, drive back up Frog Pond Road. If you wish to climb Mount Zion, turn right on St. Jean Road and take the first left onto a narrow dirt road. Drive ahead on the narrow road that leads to the left of the blue house and in 0.5 mile pass through a fence. Park in the field on your left. Walk to the small home ahead and take one of the maps of Mount Zion set out by the kindly owner of the home, and of the mount, who welcomes visitors. The trails up Zion can be challenging, and are of varying length and difficulty. Allow at least an hour for the round trip up the rocky, craggy eminence. The hiker is rewarded at the bare-rock summit with the best of all views of the battlefield and a fine look down the Taconics and at nearby Pittsford Ridge. Standing there, one surely must believe that both the Americans and the British probably used this rocky vantage as a lookout, perhaps fighting for its summit. Indeed, British soldiers may well have struggled up and over Mount Zion on their way to blocking the Castleton Road.

FRANCIS MONUMENT

Returning to the Visitors Center parking lot, you may wish to cross the road into the field where the Americans took their final position behind a farmer's long log fence. No trace remains. Back in the parking lot, look to the timberline to the north, on the far side of the field surrounding the Visitors Center. It is likely that von Riedesel's soldiers, who also saved the day for the British at Saratoga, appeared from that direction to hit the American right flank. Then gaze east to high Pittsford Ridge, over which many Americans escaped.

Directions

From the Hubbardton parking lot, turn left, north, on Monument Hill Road. This road three times crosses the route of the old military road used by St. Clair's retreating army and the pursuing British and Germans. Descending from the hills of East Hubbardton, pause a moment on reaching VT 30. The fields just ahead were known as Lacey's Camp, where Fraser's army slept briefly before continuing to Hubbardton. Turn north on VT 30 driving through picturesque lake country and 6.5 miles along turn left onto VT 73 West. Drive through attractive, ridged farm country for 5 miles and pass through the old village of Orwell. Continue on across VT 22A, proceed straight ahead at the Y onto Mount Independence Road, and follow signs to Mount Independence. In 5 miles, the road turns sharply up onto The Mount and the Visitors Center parking lot.

Mount Independence

"LOVING BROTHER, I inform you that I am & have been in a low state of health for some time past & don't imagine I shall get well very soon; wherefore I earnestly intreat you not to delay coming for me or if you can't come yourself, send a man that you can confide in & a horse for me." So wrote poor Matthew Kennedy, a soldier in the Continental

Artillery position, Mount Independence

army, in the winter of 1776–77 from the hospital at Mount Independence. His people did come, from New Hampshire, but he died before they arrived. The Mount, as it is known locally, is the resting place of hundreds of American, British, and German soldiers. Here the Americans suffered through a long winter fully as severe as Washington's troops endured at Valley Forge. And here were stationed thousands of American soldiers, manning the largest fortification built for the Revolutionary War, who turned back a British invasion in 1776.

In early July 1776, three days after the Declaration of Independence was signed, American forces evacuated Crown Point and, fearing a British advance up Lake Champlain, concentrated their defenses at Fort Ticonderoga. The decision to withdraw to there met with immediate disfavor from George Washington. But Philip Schuyler believed Ticonderoga could be made a much stronger position, with the fortifying of the rocky promontory that jutted into the lake just opposite the fort, then known as both Rattlesnake Hill and East Point. Schuyler wrote Washington that he found the place to be "so remarkably strong as to require little labor to make it tenable against a vast superiority of force, and fully to answer the purpose of preventing the enemy from penetrating into the country south of it." The place, 2 miles long and approximately 400 acres, was surrounded on three sides by water and steep banks or cliffs. Heights on the fourth side commanded all land approaches. Passing along the lake the previous year, Benjamin Franklin had also seen The Mount's strategic possibilities.

The Americans set to work constructing fortifications and on July 18, 1776, a copy of the Declaration of Independence was delivered to the American commander at Ticonderoga. Ten days later, according to the *Boston Gazette*: "Immediately after divine worship the Declaration of Independence was read by Colonel St. Clair, and having said 'God save the free independent States of America!' the army manifested their joys with three cheers. It was remarkably pleasing to see the spirits of the soldiers so raised after all their calamities; the language on every man's countenance was, 'Now we are a people! We have name among the states of the world.'"

So Rattlesnake Hill became Mount Independence and batteries, blockhouses, a hospital, a powder magazine, shops, and storehouses were constructed as well as a large star-shaped fort on its highest point. Almost all The Mount's trees were felled and campgrounds laid out. Congress authorized a maximum defensive effort and units from several colonies converged until the Ticonderoga/Independence garrison totaled 13,000 men. The British moved south in the autumn of 1776, a formidable force under Sir Guy Carleton. Hit by Benedict Arnold and his brave fleet at Valcour Island, still they came on and their armada rounded Three Mile Point, a like number of miles north of Independence, on October 28. The sight that confronted the British must have been awesome, The Mount all fortified and bristling with cannon, thousands of armed men at their posts. The British took a long look, then sent a boat toward the narrows, which was greeted with cannon fire. Carleton quickly made the decision to sail north, abandoning until spring his plans for a farther move south.

As the harsh North Country winter of 1776–77 began, the Ticonderoga/Independence garrison was reduced to 3,000 men, doing their best to survive in freezing and subzero temperatures with rations short and disease rampant. Nobody knows just how many men died or where most are buried. Despite the hardships, a mighty task began in March with the building of a bridge to connect Ticonderoga and Independence. To support the 1,600-foot-long structure, log caissons were constructed on the ice, filled with stones, then sunk to the lake bottom. Also, a huge iron chain was stretched across the lake in hopes of stopping British vessels. It was all to no avail, for in the summer of 1777 when the British returned, both The Mount and Ticonderoga continued to be poorly manned. Burgoyne landed forces on both shores, intent on outflanking the Americans. The British regulars moved up the west shore, hauling cannon to the top of Mount Defiance, or Sugarloaf Hill. Along the eastern shore came Germans with orders to cut off any American retreat.

Dr. James Thacher, with the Americans on The Mount, noted in his journal entry of July 5 "astonishment that we find the enemy have taken possession of an eminence called Sugar-loaf Hill." That night the Americans at Ticonderoga quietly crossed the bridge to Independence and St. Clair's army withdrew from The Mount, taking the military road south and east. But the American flight was revealed to the

British when an American hut somehow caught fire. Two guards manning a cannon at the bridge's east end with orders to blast any British approach were captured drunk and asleep at their posts. Simon Fraser and his men were in quick pursuit; soon they were joined by the Germans who, delayed by having to march all the way around East Creek's swamps, had narrowly missed blocking St. Clair's escape. Meanwhile, other Americans fled up the lake in boats bound for Skenesborough. The British quickly broke the cross-lake chain.

So the British again possessed Ticonderoga and they set about strengthening the fortifications on Mount Independence. In September 1777, while the armies confronted each other at Saratoga, an American force attacked Fort Ticonderoga. At the same time, some 500 American riflemen moved against Independence in a diversionary attack. The assault came from the landward side, and for a time British troops in positions commanding the southern approaches were under fire. But the Americans withdrew without making a serious assault on The Mount. By then, Mount Independence's place in history was secure.

Long known as the least disturbed of all major Revolutionary War sites, until recent years Mount Independence had been allowed to fall into ruin. Today the stone foundations of the patriots' constructions rest in the shade of trees and in the few clearings of this old place, ancient even when the American army arrived. Native Americans, far into the deep and unrecorded past, had come to The Mount for chert. Indeed, all the East Creek area is rich in prehistoric sites.

Touring Mount Independence

Visitors Center

The Visitors Center, which has a distinctly nautical design, opened at Mount Independence in the summer of 1996, is set on The Mount's southern slope near where cannon once guarded against any hostile land approach. Any visit to The Mount must begin here. A huge mural of the 2002 Ernest Haas painting of The Mount during its American fortification gives the visitor

Mount Independence is open daily, 9:30–5:30, late May through mid-October. Admission fee.

Mount Independence Visitors Center

a fine idea of how the place looked in its heyday. Two talking statues of soldiers, one an American, the other a Britisher, present two perspectives on soldiering at Independence. Workstations offer further, computerized, details on the Champlain Corridor's military campaigns. A hands-on exhibit allows children in school groups to touch artifacts. The museum displays several treasures, including two massive logs that once were part of the huge caissons that supported the Independence/ Ticonderoga Bridge. Also on prominent display is a 3,000-pound British cannon, scuttled by His Majesty's troops after they learned of Burgoyne's surrender in 1777. The huge weapon was recovered from the lake near the point of The Mount, where the British had dumped it. A Connecticut soldier's powder horn with an engraved likeness of The Mount in 1777, including the shore and horseshoe batteries, Star Fort, and bridge to Fort Ti, is displayed, along with many artifacts discovered during archaeological digs. A small theater shows a 10-minute film of The Mount's history and describes its extensive trail system.

Note: The southern portion of The Mount, including the Visitors Center, is owned by the State of Vermont. The northern end is owned by Fort Ticonderoga and is open on the above schedule and accessible from the Vermont Visitors Center.

Touring The Mount

On becoming oriented at the Visitors Center, you have nearly 6 miles of trails inviting you to explore the huge historic site. Be sure to obtain a brochure to guide your walk.

Carillon Trail

Across the road from the Visitors Center, the Carillon Trail leads past the stone remnants of a battery and blockhouse, steeply down a rocky slope to the lakeside. Along the way the trail offers fine views of the lake to the south. The tour boat *Carillon*, based at nearby Larrabee's Point, sometimes docks here to pick up passengers. Inquire at the Visitors Center for a schedule.

Southern Defenses Trail

Starting from the Visitors Center, an Americans with Disabilities Act (ADA)–accessible trail leads to The Mount's major southern fortifications. This is the one walk that should not be missed, as it leads to the defenses constructed in 1777 by the remarkable military engineer Tadeusz Kosciuszko. The batteries and infantry positions he designed, made of stone, have survived well for nearly a fourth of a millennium. Stand high within one of his batteries and the genius of Kosciuszko is readily apparent. His gun positions are three tiers high, protecting each other. Low walls provide cover for marksmen to defend the cannon from the approach of foot soldiers. Through a clearing in the trees, one sees the fields to the south of The Mount, the Hubbardton Road, and the lake beyond, making clear how the position commanded southern approaches. This is one of the loveliest places to be found at any American military site, the remnants of American fortifications preserved within a lovely wood, through which sunlight often slants. The feel of history is intense and it must be recalled that, in September 1777, when the Americans attacked Ticonderoga and Mount Independence, this position was threatened. Grapeshot and musket balls found here by archaeologists seem to prove that British troops manning these American-made works were, at least briefly, under fire.

The Red Trail

Six-tenths of a mile long and an easy walk, this trail leads to the clearly visible foundations of The Mount's general hospital, a huge two-story frame building, built in April 1777, to hold 600 patients. A long trench at one end was likely dug as the cellar for a planned expansion of the building. A well-preserved, three-sided foundation that was perhaps an officers' quarters is nearby. The trail soon reaches a lookout with a view of Mount Defiance and Fort Ticonderoga. It also passes The Mount's only gravestone, not believed to mark a soldier's grave, but likely placed in the 1800s.

Orange Trail

This 2.5-mile trail leads along high ground on the west side to the tip of Mount Independence. The trail passes through the site of the Star Fort, where its parade ground is still open and square, some say from the tramping of many soldiers' feet. The trail also passes the fort's well-preserved stone well. Soon it comes to a great pile of rocks, atop a cliff with a view toward Mount Defiance, that was once the base of a giant crane used to lift supplies from docks nearly 200 feet below. The trail passes the ruins of what are believed to have been shops where black-smiths, armorers, rope makers, wheelwrights, and other skilled craftsmen worked. High above the tip of The Mount is the mounded Horseshoe Battery, believed to have been designed by Kosciuszko, where cannon commanded the lake's narrows. The view from this American fortification to the walls of Ticonderoga is one of the grand historic views in all America, making it quickly apparent why the Ticonderoga/Independence site was so strategic. Often on summer afternoons the sounds of fife and drum drift over from Ticonderoga, so much like a time long ago. Below the battery, along the lakeshore, stands a monument erected in 1908 by the Daughters of the American Revolution honoring St. Clair's reading to his assembled troops of the Declaration of Independence. This area is surrounded by the low remnants of an earthen parapet where more cannon were mounted. The trail continues down a remnant of a road that led up The Mount from the bridge connecting Independence and Ticonderoga. It is wondrous to speculate on what personages may have walked here. Certainly they included Arnold, St. Clair, Anthony Wayne, Simon Fraser, and Kosciuszko. Along the rocky shore is the point where the eastern end of the bridge rested. Its 22 caissons still stand not far beneath the historic waters separating Independence and Ticonderoga. Farther south along the shore is the precipitous masting point, a rock outcrop from which masts were lowered onto Arnold's warships that went north to battle the British at Valcour. The place is also thought to be the site of a small 1750s French fortification, with traces of its mortared walls still in evidence. Farther along the trail are the ruins of an L-shaped foundation, perhaps a lookout's post, commanding a view of East Creek. Returning toward the Visitors Center, near the Star Fort, the trail passes the rectangular foundation of what was likely a blockhouse. Below is an area of black chert long used by Native Americans.

The Blue Trail

This pathway, 2.2 miles long, reached via the Orange or Red Trails, roughly follows a Revolutionary War supply road that connected the hospital with the bridge. On descending the old supply road toward the lake, look for American soldiers' stonework. At the base of the high cliffs is a quarry, opened in the 1750s that provided stone for Fort Carillon. Farther along the cliff's base is a large spring with stone-slab steps on which people stood to dip water. Beyond is a large grassy area where The Mount's vegetable garden was located, with traces of drainage ditches still evident. Back by the base of the cliffs are the remnants of a ramp from which supplies were hoisted by crane to the clifftop. At the trail's last stop, debris and slag indicate the location of a forge.

Directions

From The Mount Independence Visitors Center, return toward VT 22A. Just before reaching that road, turn left on VT 73. You are now skirting the north side of East Creek and the distance traveled quickly makes it obvious why Burgoyne's German soldiers were so long in

---

Note: Along The Mount's miles of trails one encounters many signs marking historic sites that are not mentioned here.

reaching Mount Independence. Eventually, wonderful views of Independence, Fort Ticonderoga, and Mount Defiance come into view, so nearby lake, but so distant by land around East Creek. Five-and-one-half miles beyond the VT 73 intersection, turn left, west, on VT 74 and in 0.5 mile you reach the ferry at Larrabee's Point. The ferry, guided by submerged cable, operates daily from May 1 to October 31. Buy a round-trip ticket. It is believed that Amherst first ordered operation of a ferry at this location in 1759. Larrabee's Point is about a mile south of where Ethan Allen and Benedict Arnold crossed the lake on the night of May 10, 1775, on their way to seize Fort Ticonderoga. The fort is visible on the bluff to the south. Along the Vermont shore by the ferry dock are signs interpreting the site's history.

Directions

From the ferry, proceed on NY 74, ignoring direction signs to Fort Ticonderoga. Cross NY 22, pass a triangular traffic island, and turn left on Cossey Street, then left onto Mount Defiance Street, and turn right at its end. Drive uphill on a narrow paved road to the top of Mount Defiance. Park and walk a few steps to the pavilion on the summit, where you will find interpretive signs.

Note: The Fort Ticonderoga Ferry does not operate in the late fall and the winter and, if closed, it is necessary to drive to Chimney Point and cross Lake Champlain on the Champlain Bridge. Then proceed down NY 9N to Ticonderoga, and after your visit there, return to Crown Point.

Chapter Eight

Fort Ticonderoga

MOUNT DEFIANCE

No matter how many times one visits Mount Defiance (Sugarloaf), the sight is always breathtaking. Indeed, as a view of American military history it may be rivaled only by the vista from Little Round Top at Gettysburg. From here Robert Rogers spied on the French at Ticonderoga. Almost directly below lies the star-shaped fort, the restored stone bastion standing on a point of land protruding into the long lake. Across the narrows is another point, wooded Mount Independence in Vermont. Right at the base of Defiance is the mouth of the LaChute River, Lake George's outflow. Looking down at the Ticonderoga Peninsula, one notices a wooded rise to the left of the fort, the Heights of Carillon, scene of the bloody battle of 1758. John Burgoyne brought cannon to Defiance's undefended summit in 1777 to help drive St. Clair's Americans from their fortifications below. And John Brown seized this hilltop from the British two months later and bombarded the fort. A shell killed a soldier on the fort's parade ground. Often, one may hear the sounds of fife and drum, and an occasional musket shot, from the fort, emphasizing its nearness.

Mount Defiance is open to the public free of charge.

Fort Ticonderoga and Mount Independence from Mount Defiance

Directions

Return from Mount Defiance via Defiance and Cossey streets to NY 22. Turn onto NY 74 and soon on the right the brick former telephone building that is now Fort Ticonderoga's research center comes in view.

Thompson-Pell Research Center

The facility welcomes the serious researcher by appointment and houses one of the world's principal collections concerning the 18th-century wars for empire. Ticonderoga has been collecting since 1909 and its storage vaults house racks of 18th-century muskets and 18th-century and War of 1812 uniforms. The center has a 13,000-volume library. Portraits of the Marquis de Montcalm and General Abercromby adorn the library walls, two men now side by side who commanded opposing forces in the bloodiest battle of the French and Indian War.

Macintosh Barn

Just beyond the research center, notice a slate-roofed barn set back in the trees. The barn is believed to have been constructed on the foundation of the structure from which Colonel John Brown rescued American prisoners during his attack on Ticonderoga on September 18, 1777. The barn is private property.

Directions

Just beyond the research center is the stone gateway to Fort Ticonderoga. Proceed through the gate as tickets are obtained at the Visitors Center a mile beyond.

FORT TICONDEROGA

No fort anywhere in the world has a history richer than that possessed by Fort Ticonderoga, yet its active life was but a score of years. Six times armies marched against the little fort in the course of twenty years; twice it held but thrice it fell. No other fort in history can boast of such a record. Such was Ticonderoga, the key to the vital Champlain Valley. —historian Edward Hamilton.

Native Americans had known Ticonderoga for thousands of years before Samuel de Champlain ventured up the lake in 1609 with a party of Algonquins and Hurons. Fort Ticonderoga makes a strong case, supported by the late historian Samuel Eliot Morison, that in a battle on the beach below where the fort now stands Champlain fired his arquebus and killed three Iroquois chiefs.

Fort Ticonderoga is open 9–5, May 10 through late October. Admission fee.

French soldiers arrived here in 1666 to build a "fortin," a little fort, that was abandoned when peace was made with the Iroquois. In 1755, early in the French and Indian War, both France and England prepared for a final struggle by building major forts, France at Ticonderoga, England at the Great Carrying Place (Fort Edward) on the Hudson. Robert Rogers, having completed a scouting trip reported: "I was within a mile of Ticonderoga fort where I endeavored to reconnoiter the enemy's walls and strength. They were engaged in raising the walls of the fort and in erecting a large blockhouse near the southeast corner of the fort with ports in it for cannon. East of the blockhouse was a battery which I imagine commanded the lake."

The French called the place Fort Carillon, a corruption of the name of a Spanish fur trader, Philippe de Carrion, who had served with the first French regulars assigned to New France, in the 1660s. Ticonderoga is a Mohawk name meaning "the land between two great waters."

In 1756, Marquis de Montcalm took command of the French army in Canada. At Ticonderoga in the summer of 1757, he prepared to mount an assault on Fort William Henry, which, though he did not know it, had been weakened when many of its troops were sent to besiege Louisburg in Nova Scotia. The French commander assembled 8,000 regulars and Canadians with 1,000 Indians, and, on July 30, he moved south against Fort William Henry. The result, of course, was the capture of the English fort, with the resulting massacre.

In 1758, it was Britain's turn to mount an expedition as the indecisive Gen. James Abercromby, called "Nabbycromby" by his troops, advanced on Ticonderoga from Fort Edward. With him was Lord Howe, illegitimate grandson of the king. The 34-year-old Howe, unlike most of his fellow officers, appreciated the spirited colonials for their abilities as wilderness fighters, especially admired Robert Rogers, and had accompanied the rangers on raiding parties. The young nobleman was immensely popular with the troops.

Montcalm, at Fort Carillon, was desperately trying to coax supplies and men from the government in time to withstand the expected attack. "I have to deal with a formidable army," Montcalm wrote, "Nevertheless I do not despair. My troops are good. From the enemy's slowness I can see that he wavers. If . . . he gives me time to establish myself on the ground I have selected on the Heights of Carillon and to entrench myself there, I shall beat them." Montcalm had decided not to allow the British to attack the fort itself and he built defenses well outside the fort stretching across the Ticonderoga Peninsula.

On July 5, a massive flotilla of more than 1,000 boats bearing Abercromby's 15,000-man army moved north along Lake George. Francis Parkman wrote: "From front to rear the line was six miles long . . . the flash of oars and glitter of weapons . . . the notes of bugle, trumpet, bagpipe and drums, answered and prolonged by a hundred woodland echoes."

In the British force, with the 42nd Regiment of Foot (The Highland Regiment), known as the Black Watch, was Major Duncan Campbell of Inverawe, Scotland. Sixteen years before, in the Highlands, a man covered with blood had come to the door of Campbell's Highland home. Saying that he was being closely pursued, the stranger implored, "Swear on your dirk you will not give me up." Campbell hid the man in his castle and, almost at once, two men arrived with the news that a Campbell cousin had been murdered. Realizing that the man he had hidden was the killer, but true to his word, Duncan Campbell said nothing. That night and the next, Campbell was awakened by his cousin's ghost crying, "Inverawe, Inverawe, blood has been shed, shield not the murderer!" On going to the stranger's hiding place, Campbell was reminded of his oath. On the third night the ghost appeared once more saying, "Farewell, Inverawe, til we meet at Ticonderoga!" Campbell had no idea of the word's meaning, but years later while serving with the Black Watch in North America, he learned to his astonishment that the Highlanders would be attacking a French fort the English called Ticonderoga! The Campbell story was preserved by Robert Louis Stevenson in an 1887 article for *Scribner's Magazine*, written while he was being treated for tuberculosis in the Adirondack resort town of Saranac Lake.

At five in the morning on July 6, 1758, advance units of regulars led by Howe and Rogers landed at a cove on the west shore of Lake George. Moving toward the fort, the 4,000 men came upon a party of French scouts. Shots rang out from the trees and Howe fell at the first salvo, shot though the heart. The next day, July 7, Abercromby ordered his dispirited army back to the landing place, giving Montcalm time to finish his breastworks. The wall of logs, according to Montcalm " . . . was formed by felling trunks of trees one upon the other and others felled in front, their branches cut and sharpened produced the effect of a chevaux-de-frise," the 18th-century equivalent of barbed wire.

Montcalm, with only a week's supply of food, certainly could not have survived a lengthy siege. But he was spared that as Abercromby, fearing the arrival of French reinforcements, suddenly ordered a frontal attack. On the morning of July 8, drums rolled and fifes screamed as redcoated British regulars, rangers, and provincial troops marched against the French breastworks. Out in open ground on the Carillon heights, as they struggled to penetrate the obstructions, the British were easy targets for French musketmen and cannoneers.

Late in the day, the Black Watch joined the assault, marching against the French lines to the beat of drums and wail of bagpipes. Though some of the Scotsmen reached, and even entered, the formidable works, they, too were slaughtered. By the end of the bloody day, six British advances had failed and Abercromby finally called a halt to the carnage. Major Duncan Campbell lay mortally wounded among the 2,000 killed or wounded in the attacking force. The French loss was fewer than 400 men. Not until the Civil War would America see such slaughter in one battle. Memories are long in the Black Watch and in recent years while the regiment was on an American tour, a regimental piper about to march into a New Hampshire arena inquired of a bystander, "Is Ticonderoga nearby?" When told it was but a hundred miles distant, he replied, "We fell like leaves there."

The night after the battle, Abercromby's broken army began a disorderly retreat. Montcalm's men spent the next day burying the dead and killing the wounded with hatchets. The French commander ordered a *Te Deum* sung on July 12 to give thanks for victory and later raised a large wooden cross, painted red, along the battlements on the Heights of Carillon.

A year later, with the competent Gen. Jeffery Amherst in command, the British returned to besiege Ticonderoga. Amherst led 9,000 men, supported by 51 pieces of heavy artillery. Chevalier de Bourlamaque, left in charge of Carillon, kept up a continuous cannonade while the British dug trenches ever closer to the fort. Amherst was just positioning his cannon when French deserters ran toward the British shouting that the fort was abandoned, though gunpowder had been set to blow it up. Amherst offered 100 guineas to any man willing to cut the fuses. There were no takers, and a thunderous explosion soon shook the earth as the powder magazine and the King's storehouse went up in smoke. Next morning, what was left of the fort was in British hands and it burned for three days.

During the next decade-and-a-half, the British allowed the fort to deteriorate. Still, when the American Revolution began in 1775, rebel officials acted quickly to seize this most strategic place. Benedict Arnold galloped to Bennington armed with a commission authorizing him to "march to the Fort at Ticonderoga and use your best endeavors to reduce the same." Arnold found Col. Ethan Allen of Vermont's Green Mountain Boys at the Catamount Tavern already assembling men for the same purpose. After considerable discussion, the two agreed to lead together the first offensive action of the Revolution.

The night of May 9, 1775, at Hands Cove on the Vermont shore, 83 men climbed into boats and rowed quietly across Champlain to beach north of the fort. At sunrise, Allen's and Arnold's force burst through the fort's wicket gate. Allen stormed up the stairs to the commander's quarters, with Arnold at his side. "Come out of there, you dammed old rat!" roared Allen. A bewildered half-clothed lieutenant named Jocelyn Feltham asked on whose authority Ethan had entered the King's fort. "In the name of the Great Jehovah and the Continental Congress," was the answer. Ticonderoga had changed hands again.

In the summer of 1775, the Ticonderoga Peninsula became a staging area for the ill-fated Canadian invasion organized by Philip Schuyler and led by Richard Montgomery, during which Ethan Allen led his abortive raid on Montréal and ended up a prisoner.

Nothing went well for the Americans in the winter of 1775–76 save for the successful transport to Boston of cannon captured at Ticonderoga and Crown Point. Henry Knox, a stout, 25-year-old Boston bookseller, in one of the amazing feats of the Revolution, delivered 59 guns to General Washington in time to force the British from his city. In wintry December 1775, Knox and his men began the journey by manhandling the cannon from the forts to the portage around the Lachute's waterfalls. Dragged up and across the steep portage, they were reloaded onto bateaux and barges, ferried up Lake George, and once more unloaded. Awaiting the cannon at Fort George for the long haul were sledges, 81 yoke of oxen, and 41 pairs of horses. Knox arrived in Cambridge on January 18. Washington placed the guns on Dorchester Heights and the British departed Boston on March 17, still celebrated in Boston as "Evacuation Day."

Meanwhile, the ambitious Canadian Campaign had failed as the demoralized American army straggled back south to Crown Point and Ticonderoga. The dismal conditions at Ticonderoga in the late summer of 1776 caused Colonel Anthony Wayne to state: "I believe it to be the ancient Golgotha or place of skulls—they are so plenty here that our people for want of other vessels drink out of them, whilst the soldiers make tent pegs of the shin and thigh bones of Abercrombie's men."

Philip Schuyler, commanding the northern army, now made plans to abandon Crown Point and to develop additional defenses at the narrow chokepoint of the lake by fortifying Mount Independence, the high peninsula opposite Ticonderoga.

From Canada, British commander Sir Guy Carleton moved south in early October 1776. After battling Benedict Arnold's little fleet at Valcour Island, Carleton approached Fort Ticonderoga in mid-October, saw the redoubts and batteries on both sides of the lake well manned, and decided to withdraw to Canada for the winter.

Anthony Wayne was now in command of a depleted Ticonderoga garrison and in February he ordered work begun on a bridge linking Ti and Independence. An outpost on Mount Hope was kept manned, overlooking the carry between the two lakes, and two blockhouses were garrisoned on Lake George's northern end. But Sugarloaf, the steep hill just west of the fort, remained undefended even though John Trumbull and the engineer Kosciuszko had urged that it be fortified. It was much too steep, their superiors argued, for cannon to be hauled up.

With the coming of spring 1777, Wayne joined Washington at Morristown and was replaced by Arthur St. Clair on June 12. Also, John Burgoyne had replaced Carleton as leader of the British invasion force advancing from Canada. The British appeared in early July and promptly seized the Mount Hope outwork. Then Burgoyne ordered cannon to the top of Defiance. Meanwhile, Burgoyne's German mercenaries made their slow way down the lake's east shore, moving to cut the Mount Independence garrison's escape route.

Few guns were to be fired however, for St. Clair noticed alarming activity on Defiance and knew what it meant. That evening, American troops began streaming over the bridge, across Mount Independence, and down the military road toward Hubbardton. When the news reached London, King George was said to have rushed into the Queen's bedchamber shouting, "I have beat them! I have beat all the Americans!"

Burgoyne moved south, leaving only two regiments to man the fort, Mount Independence, and the outlying batteries and blockhouses. However, the British occupation was not to be a peaceful one. In mid-September, as Burgoyne and Gates confronted each other at Saratoga, Gen. Benjamin Lincoln sent a force from Vermont toward Ticonderoga to cut off Burgoyne's chain of supply and communication back to Canada. Colonel John Brown (no relation to the abolitionist) seized a barn near Ticonderoga and released more than 100 prisoners, also capturing 300 British soldiers. Then he attacked and seized Mount Defiance, hauled cannon to the top, and fired into the fort for two days. Brown also seized the old "French Lines" from the previous war and sent a note to the fort's commander, Brig.-Gen. H. Watson Powell, demanding surrender. Powell flatly refused and Brown thought the better of making an all-out try. An advance against Mount Independence fared no better. When Brown withdrew he also seized a number of British boats. The British held The Mount and Ticonderoga until Burgoyne's surrender.

The war dragged on, yet as it became apparent that a peace treaty would eventually be signed, in 1783 Washington decided to make a tour of the northern war zone. Reaching Lake George, he and Philip Schuyler were rowed down to Ticonderoga's carry, from whence these senior officers inspected the fort whose 1777 surrender had so distressed them.

To escape Philadelphia's summer heat in 1791, two other distinguished Americans, Thomas Jefferson and James Madison, made the northern tour. "I have often projected (a northern journey . . . as a) gratification for my curiosity." Madison wrote. After touring Saratoga, he noted, "We have also visited Forts William Henry and George,

Ticonderoga, Crown Point, which have been scenes of blood from a very early part of our history."

After the war, Fort Ticonderoga was turned over to New York State, which transferred the property to the Regents of the University of the State of New York. Columbia University and Union Colleges, in effect, shared the property. William Ferris Pell, a merchant with interests both in Montréal and New York, had admired the picturesque ruins as he traveled the lake. In 1820 he bought Fort Ticonderoga, built a summer home adjacent to it, and established a garden where French soldiers had once cultivated and planted. Today, nearly two centuries later, the Pell family is still dedicated not only to preserving the fort, but to sharing its history with the public.

Touring Ticonderoga

On entering the fort grounds off NY 74 (at the historical boundary of General Amherst's "garrison grounds" 1,500 yards from the flag bastion of the fort) through stone gates, the visitor comes upon one of America's great battlefields. Here, on the Heights of Carillon, in 1758, General Abercromby sent repeated attacks against the fort's defenses. Soon, the French outer works come in view, walls of rammed earth and logs still impressively high, with artillery embrasures clearly visible. Beside the road is a large stone cairn that contains stones from the Scottish Highlands, dedicated by the Black Watch Regiment in 1997. A marker states: SACRED TO THE MEMORY THE GALLANT HIGHLANDERS OF THE 42ND REGIMENT OF FOOT, "THE BLACK WATCH." FROM A REGIMENT A THOUSAND STRONG 205 DIED AND 287 WERE WOUNDED JULY 8, 1758, ASSAULTING THE FRENCH LINES ON THE HEIGHTS OF CARILLON. THEIR GLORY SHALL NEVER DIE. While Abercromby attacked all along the mile-long French lines, the Black Watch assaulted to the left, or north, of the present road. Remarkably, a few of the Highlanders managed to breach, briefly, the French lines. A year later, when the British returned under Amherst, the small French force withdrew to the fort itself. Amherst used these lines for protection as he laid siege to the fort. Look along the road for two square iron railings that protect impact holes made by French mortar shells fired against Amherst's troops.

In 1776, American soldiers strengthened the old French lines in preparing to defend Ticonderoga against the advance of Sir Guy Carleton. The lines were again manned by the Americans in 1777 when Burgoyne assaulted the fort. That fall, John Brown's men captured and briefly held these works.

Drive through the lines and one immediately sees, to the right, a replica of the red-painted cross Montcalm erected in 1758. Proceeding toward the fort, a marker informs that American campsites from 1776–77 survive in the nearby woods. Nearing the fort, note two American redoubts to the left. Near the parking lot and another 1776 American redoubt, a marker points to a cemetery where men who died during the American occupation of 1775–77 are buried.

Visitors Center

The fort's 1930s Visitors Center, of log construction, contains a gift shop, bookstore, and restaurant. Purchase admission tickets here.

THE FORT

From the Visitors Center, proceed into the fort walking at the base of its massive stone walls. Once a ruin, the fort has since 1909 been faithfully reconstructed. On passing through the arched gateway, note the plaque that reads: THROUGH THE ENTRANCE TO THE PLACE D'ARMES OF THE FORT HAVE PASSED: GEORGE WASHINGTON, BENJAMIN FRANKLIN, BENEDICT ARNOLD, HORATIO GATES, ANTHONY WAYNE, ARTHUR ST. CLAIR, HENRY KNOX, PHILIP SCHUYLER, RICHARD MONTGOMERY, SETH WARNER, MAJOR ROBERT ROGERS, THE MARQUIS DE MONTCALM, JOHN BURGOYNE, THADEUS KOSCIUSZKO, THE DUC DE LEVIS, SIR JEFFERY AMHERST, SIR GUY CARLETON, MAJOR JOHN ANDRE AND A HOST OF OTHER GREAT MEN OF OUR HISTORY. YOU WHO TREAD IN THEIR FOOTSTEPS REMEMBER THEIR GLORY.

Entering the parade ground, look to the left, to the West Barracks. The staircase on the left was ascended by Ethan Allen and Benedict

Arnold in the early hours of May 10, 1775, to demand the fort's surrender. Ticonderoga has one of the world's largest collections of cannon and the two directly opposite on the parade ground were taken from the fort by Henry Knox to help drive the British from Boston. One made it; the other fell through the Mohawk River's ice. The parade ground once came under fire, from American cannon on Mount Defiance.

In the barracks, the life of French soldiers stationed at the fort is re-created. The men slept three to a bed in their bunks. Also in the barracks, some of the treasures of the fort's remarkable collection are displayed, including:

- Ethan Allen's pistols and the sword he carried into the fort.

- Captain de la Place's pistols.

- The blunderbuss Allen loaned to Benedict Arnold for the attack.

- Toy soldiers owned, as a boy, by General Montcalm.

- Three muskets captured by John Brown when he freed Americans imprisoned in the nearby barn.

- John Brown's Revolutionary War sword.

- A British blanket found on the Hubbardton Battlefield.

- Robert Rogers's powderhorn.

- American landscape artist Thomas Cole's first signed and dated painting, his 1826 *View Near Ticonderoga*.

- Thomas Davies's 1774 painting of Amherst's army assembled at the south end of Lake George to advance against Ticonderoga. In the painting's foreground, standing beside an Indian, is a ranger who could well be Robert Rogers.

Nicholas Westbrook is the longtime director of the fort, and his favorite item from the collection is always on display: the canvas knapsack carried by Benjamin Warner throughout the years of the Revolution. On a paper placed within the knapsack, Warner wrote:

This knapsack I cary'd through the war of the Revolution to achieve the Merican Independence. I transmit it to my oldest son, Benjamin Warner Jr. with directions to keep it and transmit it to his oldest sone and so on to the latest posterity and whilst one shred of it shall remane never surrender your libertys to a foren envador or an aspiring demagog.—Benjamin Warner, Ticonderoga, March 27, 1837

Another of the fort's treasures is the famous silver bullet in which was concealed a message from Gen. Sir Henry Clinton, in New York City, to General Burgoyne, nearing Saratoga, but carried by mistake to the Americans. Upon his capture, the messenger swallowed the bullet, but was given an emetic. When the ball emerged and its message was read, the man was hanged. The message is also preserved.

Walk the ramparts, still defended by scores of cannon. The views to Mount Defiance, up and down the lake, and to Mount Independence, are spectacular, seemingly little changed since the fort's days of glory. Look to the south, along the adjacent lakeshore, where support structures for the fort stood, including a blacksmith shop, baking ovens, a brick kiln, and a brewery. Wharves on the shore above and below the fort provided landing places for military and supply boats.

FORT TICONDEROGA

Revolutionary War battle reenactment at Fort Ticonderoga

THE PAVILION

From the Fort, proceed on foot or by car down to the Pavilion, long-time home of the Pell family. The grand old house faces the lake, and on its large front lawn is a marker at the possible site of Champlain's 1609 battle with the Iroquois. Nearby is the remarkable King's Garden, designed in 1920 by America's first woman landscape architect, Marian Cruger Coffin.

Sites Outside the Fort

Pick up a brochure at the Visitors Center to guide you to historic sites in and around the village of Ticonderoga. It seems that history happened everywhere here. Be sure to visit Mount Hope, a Fort Ticonderoga outer work about a mile from the fort's gates. Mount Hope, which protected the fort's sawmill and the carrying place that connected Lake George with Lake Champlain, was captured by Burgoyne's troops in 1777. Other sites around Ticonderoga include:

- A marker on the site of Lord Howe's death.
- Four markers along the beginning route of General Knox's trek to Boston.
- The site of British and French sawmills near the lovely falls of the LaChute River.
- Mossy Point Boat Launch near the northern end of Lake George where Abercromby's army landed in 1758, Amherst's army in 1759, and where Montcalm departed in 1757 to attack Fort William Henry.

Fort Ticonderoga is always a work in progress. The fort's east barracks will soon be reconstructed to house an education center, with a 200-seat auditorium. Its opening will make it possible for the fort to be open year-round. Also, a thorough restoration of the Pavilion, which dates to 1826, has been planned.

Directions

From Fort Ticonderoga, return to Vermont via the Larrabee's Point Ferry. From the ferry, take VT 74 east and on the left, about 1 mile along, look for a sizeable historic marker and an interpretive sign set below the road.

HANDS COVE

Nearby is Hands Cove, where Ethan Allen, Benedict Arnold, and the Green Mountain Boys set forth in rowboats the night of May 10, 1775, to capture Ticonderoga. Indeed, a portion of the cove is visible, as are Fort Ticonderoga, Mount Independence, and Mount Defiance. Hands Cove is privately owned and closed to the public.

Directions

Continue on VT 74 about 4 miles to the village of Shoreham and turn north on VT 22A. Proceed 7 miles to the village of Bridport and turn west on VT 125. Follow VT 125 a little more than 4 miles until the Crown Point Bridge comes in view. Just past an old brick farmhouse surrounded by a hedge, is a small marker for the Crown Point Road.

Chapter Ten

Crown Point
and Chimney Point

CROWN POINT ROAD

The marker states: ON THE LAKE SHORE DIRECTLY WEST GEN.
AMHERST'S MEN BEGAN BUILDING THE CROWN POINT ROAD ON AUG.
8, 1759. The Crown Point Road was created by the British to link
their fort at Crown Point with The Fort at Number Four on the Connecticut River at Charlestown, New Hampshire. The road did not
begin at Chimney Point, directly across from Crown Point, because
early settlers considered Chimney Point, surrounded by lake and wetlands, to be an island. It started, instead, more than a mile south of
Chimney Point, on dry land. The road led east out of the Champlain
Valley to Rutland and over the Green Mountains to a blockhouse on
the Connecticut River north of Springfield, Vermont. There a ferry
took travelers across the river to The Fort at Number Four. The Crown
Point Road Association maintains a series of markers along the old
road's route and publishes a guidebook. To obtain a copy, write:
  Crown Point Road Association
  51 Eden Avenue
  Proctor, Vermont 05765

Fort Crown Point

Directions

From the marker, continue on VT 125 soon passing through a marshy area, making it clear why Chimney Point was once considered to be an island. In 2 miles, turn west on VT 17 and enter the Chimney Point Historic Site on the left.

CHIMNEY POINT

Chimney Point's history can be traced back 7,500 years to when Native Americans regularly camped here. The place was first visited by Europeans in 1609, during Champlain's exploration. Early on it was known as "Pointe à la Chevelure," which some translate as "Place of Scalps." The French built a small stone fort in 1690, but it was not until 1731 that they established a settlement here, around a temporary wooden stockade they

Open Memorial Day to Columbus Day, Wednesday through Sunday, 9:30–5. Admission fee.

The tavern, Chimney Point

called "Fort de Pieux." That small fort, set on the bluff where the tavern now stands, protected French interests in the valley until a permanent fort, St. Frederic, was built across the narrows at Crown Point. By 1743, a settlement built by Seigneur Gilles Hocquart at Chimney Point constituted the largest French habitation in the Champlain Valley. Just before Jeffery Amherst drove the French from the valley in 1759, 57 French families lived in the area. Either Amherst or the departing French put the torch to any French buildings, and their chimneys, visible from Crown Point, gave the place its name.

In the summer of 1776, American forces for a time occupied Crown Point and Chimney Point. The Revolutionary War journal of engineer Jeduthan Baldwin states that on July 5, 1776, he "Laid out works on Chimny point, Genl. Schuyler, Gen. Gates & Arnold came to this place in the evening."

After the war, probably in the 1780s, a tavern was built atop the bluff where the French fort and the American works surely stood. To the place in June 1791 came Thomas Jefferson and James Madison, on their tour of northern New York and Vermont. Some said politics was their primary mission, though the writings of Jefferson reveal that he was much interested in nature. The tavern was bought by the Barnes Family in 1819, who owned it until 1969. Ambitious promoters of tourism, they added the tavern's grand porch in 1897 when they turned it into a summer resort. The Barneses boasted that the taproom dates to the Revolutionary War and that Ethan Allen planned the attack on Ticonderoga there—also that he and Remember Baker once jumped from a window to escape from the British. But recent research has shown that the tavern is not quite that old.

Touring Chimney Point

The State of Vermont Division for Historic Preservation has made a museum of the old tavern. An exhibit, including many artifacts, traces the history of Native American people in the Champlain Valley and of French settlement. A rotating exhibit of contemporary Abenaki art is also displayed and the last post office that operated in the town of Addison is preserved. Also, there is information on the ferry service that ran between Chimney Point, and Crown Point and Port Henry on the New York shore, until a bridge was built. Best of all is the perfectly preserved taproom. Its appearance dates from the very early 1800s when the building was given a face-lift. If not old enough to have a Revolutionary War history, the room bore witness to the raising of glasses by thousands of lake travelers for more than a century and a half. Jefferson and Madison surely trod the ancient floorboards the modern visitor now walks. On leaving the tavern, be sure to drive or walk down to the lakeshore, under the graceful Champlain Bridge. There you will see the stone ruins of two ferry docks. The smaller one, pointing northwest, dates to the visit of Jefferson and Madison. It's likely those two founders of the nation stepped ashore here. An interpretive sign describes the history.

Directions
Cross the high Champlain Bridge and several hundred yards beyond, turn right to enter the Crown Point Historic Site.

CROWN POINT

At Crown Point, a story comes to mind concerning a tourist who stopped one day to admire the Golden Gate Bridge arching the entrance to San Francisco Bay. "Isn't that beautiful?" he exclaimed. "You should have seen it before they built the bridge," said an old man sitting nearby.

This New York State Historic Site is open 9–5, May 1 through October 31. Admission fee.

The same sentiment about the Champlain Bridge might apply; built in 1929, it links Crown Point and Chimney Point. The high silver span considerably intrudes on one of America's great historic places. Yet, it serves as a grand entrance to the storied acreage of Crown Point and its remnants of the mighty forts of two grand empires.

It's not beyond the realm of possibility that a great gleaming stone shaft might have stood at Crown Point paying honor to George Washington—the Washington Monument. In the summer of 1783, Washington came north from his headquarters on the Hudson River on his

Champlain Bridge and Fort St. Frederic

inspection tour. He stopped at Ticonderoga, and then moved to Crown Point where he camped. Though the British had already surrendered at Yorktown, no peace treaty would be signed until three months later, and Lake Champlain still had an English presence. As Tim Titus, a former historian at the Crown Point State Historic Site, is fond of pointing out, Washington is fortunate that he was not killed or captured at Crown Point. But no British troops were around at the time and "The Father of his Country" departed unharmed.

Fort St. Frederic, with the look of a European castle, was the first major fortification completed along Lake Champlain, and for a quarter century it gave France control of the Champlain Valley. Crown Point became a place famous throughout Europe, a key outpost on the frontier of the New World. A beehive of military activity, a considerable

---

Fort St. Frederic

Crown Point became of major importance in 1734 when the king of France directed that a fortification, Fort St. Frederic, be built on the tip of the peninsula just across the waters from Chimney Point where an earlier French fort had stood. A Swede, botanist Peter Kalm, traveling the lake in 1749, described it:

> The fort is built on a rock, consisting of black-lime slates . . . it is nearly quadrangular, has high and thick walls, made of the same lime-stone of which there is a quarry about half a mile from the fort. On the eastern part of the fort is a high tower, which is proof against bombshells, provided with very thick and substantial walls, and well stored with cannon from the bottom almost to the very top; and the governor lives in the tower. In the terre-plein of the fort is a well built little church, and houses of stone for the officers and soldiers . . . Within one or two musket-shots to the east of the fort is a wind-mill built of stone, with very thick walls . . . The wind-mill is so contrived as to serve the purpose of the redoubt, and at the top of it are five or six small pieces of cannon.

settlement grew up outside its walls on both sides of the lake. From St. Frederic the military forays that sacked Falmouth, Maine, Fort Massachusetts, and Saratoga were launched. From 1755 to 1758, the British mounted four expeditions aimed at seizing Crown Point. All failed until Amherst rolled north in 1759, and the French defenders fled without a fight. But before leaving, they blew up St. Frederic's mighty stone tower.

Ten days after arriving at Crown Point, Amherst ordered construction of a new bastion, some 300 yards inland from the French fort. The general was a demon for building, so fascinated by engineering that near Crown Point he once took apart a beaver dam to see how it was constructed. His Majesty's Fort at Crown Point, constructed of earth, stone, and wood, was the largest fort ever built by the British in North America. The overall fortification complex, with several large outer works, covered three-and-one-half square miles and cost the Crown the equivalent of $10 million.

"The Fort is of wood, built in a most masterly manner," observed a British visitor in 1765. "It has five Bastions, mounts 105 guns, and has casemates for 4,000 men. Within the fort are good Stone Barracks for officers and Men which . . . would conveniently contain 500 men." The two-story limestone barracks housed between 12 and 18 soldiers in each room, warmed by a fireplace, who received clean sheets once a month, when available.

Amherst also ordered construction of a road to Fort Ticonderoga, as well as the long road to the Connecticut River. In 1760, the British expedition that captured Montréal and placed the corridor under British control moved north from the fort.

In 1773, a barracks chimney fire quickly spread to the powder magazine, causing a massive explosion and the burning of the wooden parts of the fort. With the outbreak of the American Revolution and with Amherst's once mighty fort in ruins, Seth Warner and a small detachment of rebels walked in the day after Ethan Allen seized Ticonderoga and made Crown Point American property. Cannon taken from the great fort's ruins went with Knox to Boston. From Crown Point the American expedition, aimed at conquering Canada, was launched in 1775. And to Crown Point the next June came the remnants of that expedition, defeated and riddled with smallpox. In the autumn of 1776, Carleton and his large British army camped at Crown Point. American forces regained control of the peninsula after Carleton's departure, even building a new fortification at Coffin Point, south of Crown Point on a bluff overlooking the lakeshore. The next summer, the British came again, this time led by Burgoyne.

Touring Crown Point

Entrance

Immediately across the highway from the site entrance is a partially preserved redoubt, called the Light Infantry Redoubt, a part of the English fort's outer defenses. A view of the British fort's ramparts, with the great stone chimneys of its barracks rising above, commands the curving drive to the Site Museum. Beyond rise the distinctive, rounded hills across Bulwaga Bay, which early artists depicting Crown Point loved to portray, and to exaggerate. On the right, just before reaching the stone picnic pavilion, look for a gentle, grassy rise of earth, an outwork of the French fort.

Site Museum

Located between the two forts and commanding a fine view north along the lake, this small facility offers a wealth of information on Crown Point. A small theater shows a somewhat dated, but informative, slide show on Crown Point's history. An electric map describes a walking tour of the area. Of particular interest are detailed models of Fort St. Frederic and Fort Crown Point. Look for the tiny British soldiers in and about the British fort model that demonstrates well the structure's massive size. A sketch of Fort St. Frederic is etched on a window facing its ruins, cleverly positioned so that it may be viewed as it was in its days of glory. Among the museum's treasures is a limestone keystone from Fort St. Frederic; a small, swivel-mounted French cannon called a "Pierrier," found in the ruins of the French fort; a British 12-pounder cannon captured at Fort William Henry by the

French; and a 1761 powder horn on which a British soldier carved a likeness of His Majesty's fort here.

French Fort

Using a brochure from the museum, walk first to the French fort. Note that as you enter the place, you cross a dry moat where the fort's draw-bridge was once located. The pile of stone and earth along the east side of the parade ground are the remains of the four-story fortified tower, which once mounted cannon. Also visible are the foundations of the fort's chapel and portions of its brick bakery ovens. Just north of the fort is a covered way, dug through earth and stone, giving the French defenders in the event of attack a protected route to the lakeshore. Take a long look at this ancient place before passing on. Here the white flag of France once waved over a mighty fortress that gave the French Empire control of Lake Champlain.

British Fort

The walking tour leads to the still formidable British fort and the experience of entering the old parade ground never fails to amaze. The thick walls still rise on all sides to a most impressive height, enclosing a massive open space within which the stone walls of two barracks stand. Explore the remnants of the officers' and enlisted men's quarters, some of which have preserved fireplaces. It is easy to imagine the loneliness of the troops, an ocean away from home in a strange land. Go to the fort's deep well, and look into the mighty moat that surrounded the vast structure. Climb atop the fort's walls and see the depressions where cannon once were mounted. Looking to the southwest, you'll see the rather level area where a British village stood, and most of the fort's garrison lived. Proceed in that direction; the limestone upon which you walk was once the bottom of a vast inland salt sea millions of years ago. British excavations that provided dirt for the fort's walls exposed the ancient rock. Some 500 yards out, following the mown trail, see on high ground to the left the ramparts of a redoubt, once manned by His Majesty's 80th Regiment of Light Infantry. When you stand on its walls and look back at the main fort, you will better understand why Amherst once said this stronghold was the most defensible in North America.

Directions

Driving out of the historic site, note on the left as you near the entrance the level grasslands that once were the big fort's gardens. Turn left and then right into the New York State camping area.

CHAMPLAIN MEMORIAL LIGHTHOUSE

The stone tower by the lake is a monument built around an old lighthouse that stood on the site of a fortified windmill that was part of Fort St. Frederic's defenses. The stonework around and below the tower is the remains of another major outwork of the British fort. The monument, built by the states of New York and Vermont, honors Samuel de Champlain. Indeed, Crown Point historians believe that Champlain fought the Iroquois not at Ticonderoga, but somewhere along the Crown Point shore. The observation deck offers a fine view of the historic site, the lake, and particularly of Vermont mountains. One well understands from here why both British and French thought of the lake south of Crown Point as a river.

The camping area is open May 1 through Columbus Day. A Crown Point State Historic Site ticket gains admission here.

High on the lakeside of the structure is a monumental bronze statue of a powerful Champlain, accompanied in canoe by an Indian and a French soldier, making his way up the long lake. Beneath that sculpture, and unnoticed by many visitors, is a small bronze bust of a young woman. Known as *La France*, it is the work of the great French sculptor Auguste Rodin. The Memorial Lighthouse was constructed as part of the huge celebration that took place in 1909 around the 300th anniversary of Champlain's discovery of Lake Champlain. Completed in 1912, the memorial was dedicated that year and the Rodin was presented by the French government. Speaking at the dedication of the refurbished memorial in 1959, Congressman (and later New York City mayor) John Lindsay said, "Rodin's *La France* was the spontaneous gift of the French people to America on the celebration 50 years ago of the 300th anniversary of Champlain's discovery. One of the corridor's treasures, it is a magnificent creation, done in bronze and permanently set in the base of the monument, facing the water. This monument, therefore, is a noble testimony to the friendship of two great nations." Rodin seems to portray a look of wonder on the face of *La France* on seeing for the first time the grand valley and lake that would one day bear the name Champlain.

Landing Place

On the lakeshore, between the bridge and the Champlain monument, is Crown Point's landing place, where the British moved north against Montréal and Montcalm moved south against Fort William Henry. From this beach Burgoyne and Carleton pointed their armies toward Ticonderoga. Also, it's likely that Washington and Franklin landed here. Crown Point historian Tom Nesbitt is fond of noting that in addition to French and British forts, an American fort once stood nearby. Its location, south of the Memorial Lighthouse, is at a place that old maps may identify as Coffin Point. Nobody seems to know the origin of the name. For decades a resort was located at Coffin Point, a destination for vacationers well into the 20th century. On entering the site of the old resort, you can see a wall of the 1776 American fort and its southern bastion. The fort is within a restricted area on State of New York land. But Nesbitt can sometimes be persuaded to escort a visitor to the fort whose history he continues to research.

On leaving Crown Point, glance back from the high bridge and you'll see the French and British flags flying in the lake's winds and breezes, and feel the power of this once, and still, mighty place.

Directions
From the Visitors Center parking lot, return across the Champlain Bridge. Turn left on VT 17 East and quickly cross Hospital Creek.

Hospital Creek

The name Hospital Creek goes back to 1759, when General Amherst moved his sick soldiers across the narrow lake in order to isolate them from the rest of his army. The American army that returned to Crown Point in June 1776 from the failed invasion of Canada was infected by smallpox and some of its sick were transported here, though most were taken to the hospital at Fort George. John Trumbull wrote: "At this place I found not an army but a mob, the shattered remains of twelve or fifteen very fine battalions, ruined by sickness, fatigue, and desertion, and void of every idea of discipline or subordination . . . We now have three thousand sick." That sorry condition persisted only a short time, for the decision was soon made to withdraw to Fort Ticonderoga and Mount Independence.

Directions

Hospital Creek is surrounded by private property and may only be viewed from the highway. The locations of the hospitals are unknown, though they were likely near the mouth of the creek. Continue north on VT 17 for 1 mile and turn left into the Strong House Museum.

THE STRONG HOUSE

Open 10–5, Saturday and Sunday, Memorial Day through Labor Day, and during fall foliage season. Admission fee.

This graceful brick house is a monument to frontier survival, strong as the Strong family that survived wilderness hardships to build it. John Strong, his wife Agnes, and their three children came to this location from Connecticut in the winter of 1776 and built a cabin. The first year in this northern wilderness, the Strongs were plagued by meddlesome bears. The following summer, as Burgoyne's expedition neared, and with her husband away, Agnes was warned by a neighbor to flee, for Indians were approaching. Though in poor health, she managed to

The Strong House

grab a few belongings and, putting the youngest child in a sack on the back of her oldest boy, she fled south along the lakeshore. Arriving at the mouth of Hospital Creek, the Strongs barely caught the last departing boat. It took them all the way to Skenesborough and, weeks later, the entire family was reunited. On returning, they found their home burned but decided to stay and built this handsome brick house.

Touring the house

Members of the Vermont Daughters of the American Revolution escort visitors through the house. The brick federal structure is filled with period furnishings. Of particular interest is the stone walk-in fireplace. The iron fireplace crane was recovered from the ashes of the original Strong cabin. On an upstairs wall is artist Julian Scott's excellent painting of Ethan Allen's men assembling at Hand's Cove for the capture of Ticonderoga. Another treasure is a sword reportedly captured by those men at Fort Ti. Be sure to visit the lovely, and lovingly tended, garden in the rear of the house. The foundation of the original Strong dwelling may be seen in the DAR State Park adjacent to the Strong House.

Directions

From the Strong House, continue north on VT 17 for 0.5 mile and bear to the left off VT 17 where the road divides at a store. Proceed 5.5 miles following the lakeshore where the road turns sharp right, turn left onto Pease Road, and in 0.2 mile come to a marker noting that Arnold's Bay is nearby. Continue 0.5 mile to the four-way intersection, turn left on Adams Ferry Road, and go to its end beyond the Vergennes Water District Plant at a landing on the lakeshore.

Chapter Eleven

Arnold's Bay
to the Maritime Museum

ARNOLD'S BAY

"I've always had this image of Arnold, his men, and the Ferris family running off through the fields with the grapeshot falling everywhere. It was all through those fields." Those are the words of archaeologist Starbuck who in 1988 conducted an excavation at the remains of the Ferris House, which overlook Arnold's Bay. Not surprisingly, he found a quantity of British grapeshot in the field around the Ferris House, for the place was once under fire from British gunboats.

It happened on October 13, 1776, two days after Arnold battled the British fleet at Valcour. Fleeing south, the little American force was gradually overtaken. Historian Hill wrote:

> Having sailed and rowed his battered and leaking vessels all night after the battle, Arnold was forced to sink two of his gondolas near Schuyler Island. Further time was sacrificed plugging leaks, mending sails, and, on the second sleepless night, bucking fickle winds. With the sails scarcely filled off Willsboro on the morning of the 13th, and with the British catching up because of still-conflicting winds, Arnold gradually lost hope of beating them to Crown Point—although the schooner

Revenge, the sloop *Enterprise*, the galley *Trumbull*, and one gondola managed to do so. Almost overtaken north of Split Rock, the galley *Lee* was run into a bay on the east shore. The shattered *Washington* had suffered so many killed and wounded that General Waterbury struck her colors after receiving another battering. The gondola *Jersey* also surrendered.

Arnold said that he was then attacked by a ship with twelve 18-pounders aboard, a schooner with six 14-pound guns, and another ship with twelve 6-pounders that closed to within musket range. The hull, sails, and rigging of the *Congress* were mangled, he said, and to prevent her capture, he ran her into the shore "in a small creek 10 miles from Crown Point, on the east side."

So Arnold landed at this bay, a place that would later be named for him, set fire to his boats, and went up the steep embankment where he and his men were under fire for a time from British boats anchored just outside the bay. They then set out overland to American-held Crown Point and safety. A sizeable house stood on the bluff overlooking the bay, owned by farmer Peter Ferris, in which he operated a tavern. Ferris and his family fled with Arnold.

With Arnold's hasty departure, the British came ashore and destroyed the Ferris farm. The Ferrises returned and resumed their lives on the bay, until their buildings were again burned, by British raiders, who took Peter Ferris and a son to Québec where they were imprisoned. They returned in 1782 to resume farming and begin a ferry service from Arnolds Bay.

It should also be noted that on April 24, 1775, a boat bearing the commission sent to assess the American invasion of Canada put in at Arnold's Bay for the night, perhaps disembarking on the stone pier that sometimes protrudes from the water just off the Ferris site. Benjamin Franklin and associates passed the evening at the Ferris home, and next day resumed their way north. In late fall 1859, the sad little procession bearing the body of John Brown came to Arnold's Bay. Having passed through Vergennes, the casket accompanied by his widow Mary Ann Brown, was brought to Adams Ferry, which operated between the bay and Westport, New York. From Westport, they began the long climb into the Adirondacks to the Brown home at North Elba. The vantage point by the water-treatment plant is the site

Arnold's Bay

of the ferry landing. Despite local discontent with his decision, the Rev. Joshua Young, of Burlington, agreed to officiate at Brown's funeral and came here to take the Adams Ferry on his way to North Elba. But on reaching Arnold's Bay, the reverend encountered a severe storm that had put the ferry out of operation. After a wait, in the night the weather suddenly cleared. "God's full-orbed moon has thrown a bridge of silver across the lake," Young told the ferryman, and the crossing was made.

Touring Arnold's Bay

The point of land by the water-treatment plant provides a good view of the bay. Look to the far side of the bay and you will see a white fence on the bluff. With your eye, follow the fence to its left end, and note that the bluff drops off to the mouth of a creek. Where the bluff resumes, what is left of the stone foundation of the Ferris House lies in a stand of sumac, and spills down toward the shore. The Ferris House site is on private property and closed to the public. The British ships were firing from quite near where you stand. One can imagine

Arnold's men scrambling up the steep bluffs and through the fields beyond.

Directions

From Arnold's Bay, return to the four-way intersection and turn left, or north. The old graveyard on the left contains the grave of Peter Ferris and his family, in its southwest corner. Proceed 1.5 miles to the end of the road that turns to gravel and turn left on paved Button Bay Road. The bay is on your left.

Button Mold Bay

Also known as Button Bay, this handsome inlet is named for the strange button-shaped stones that cover its shores. Arnold brought his little fleet into the bay on August 24, 1776, on his way to Valcour, forced to seek refuge from a storm. On June 24, 1777, Burgoyne's army of nearly 8,000 camped here.

LAKE CHAMPLAIN MARITIME MUSEUM

Directions

Continue past the bay, and turn left on Basin Harbor Road. Proceed 0.5 mile to the parking lot of the Lake Champlain Maritime Museum.

Located on North Harbor, adjacent to Basin Harbor, neither of which has a significant military history, the Lake Champlain Maritime Museum nonetheless has assembled a formidable array of Champlain Corridor history at its lakeshore campus. The place includes 12 exhibit buildings, a full-sized replica of Benedict Arnold's gunboat the *Philadelphia*, an archaeology conservation laboratory where the work may be viewed in progress, boat building and blacksmithing demonstrations, and playgrounds and picnic areas. The museum has excellent exhibits explaining the military history of Lake Champlain.

Open daily 10–5, May 3 through mid-October. Admission fee.

Touring the museum

Be sure to visit the exhibit Key to Liberty: the Revolutionary War in the Champlain Valley. Included are:

- a 4-pounder cannon and a swivel gun recovered from Arnold's Bay, believed to have been tossed overboard from Arnold's ships.
- two frames from an Arnold vessel, the *Congress*.
- an anchor likely from one of Arnold's boats.
- the stem post from an Arnold gunboat, the *New York*.
- models of the *Philadelphia* and the row galley, the *Washington*, that fought at Valcour.

Videos are shown on the recovery of the *Philadelphia* from near Valcour Island, the building of the replica *Philadelphia II* at the Maritime Museum, and on the discovery of the last of Arnold's boats to be located, the gunboat, *Spitfire*. A film, *Key to Liberty*, deals with the Battle of Valcour Island, emphasizing Arnold's service to the United States.

An exhibit on underwater archaeology includes an anchor ring and shank from the *Confiance*, along with other artifacts from the 1814 battle. Also, you may watch preservation work in progress on artifacts in the conservation laboratory through a large viewing window. Workers are happy to answer questions.

The unquestioned star of the Maritime Museum is the *Philadelphia II*, an exact replica of an Arnold warship that was sent to the bottom off Valcour by British guns. The craft, fully seaworthy, is moored at a dock in North Harbor, just a short walk down to the lakeshore from the museum campus. The setting is lovely, the little harbor looking out on the Champlain Narrows and the ledges of Barn Rock's palisades on the New York shore. The harbor is just up the lake from Split Rock, where the British overtook Arnold's battered fleet on its retreat southward. Arnold sailed past the harbor's mouth, along the near shore, to put in at Arnold's Bay. Visitors are welcome aboard the 29-ton gunboat that mounts three cannon and eight swivel guns. The bow gun alone weighs 4,000 pounds. The 54-foot-long gunboat somehow managed to accommodate a crew of 44. Ask the interpreters on board just how 44 men lived in such a small space. To visit the *Philadelphia II* is to marvel at the bravery of Arnold and his men in facing a British fleet in such a small, cramped, low-riding craft.

Directions

Leaving the museum, turn left from the driveway onto Basin Harbor Road, which soon follows Otter Creek along which Macdonough brought his new fleet, bound for Plattsburgh, from Vergennes out into Lake Champlain. Tree branches had to be cut along the banks to allow the ships' masts to pass. On the far bank is the road to Fort Cassin, the fortification built by the Americans in 1814 to protect Macdonough's fleet. The fort is on private property and is not open to the public. In just under 5 miles at the end of Basin Harbor Road, turn left, and in 0.25 mile turn left again, or north, on VT 22A. Cross the Otter Creek Bridge spanning the falls of Otter Creek, go up the hill, and turn left on Macdonough Street. Quickly, on the left, is a historic site marker in a small riverside park. Here on the banks of this wide basin Macdonough built his fleet.

Chapter Twelve

Vergennes

As THE WINTER OF 1813–14 BEGAN, up Otter Creek to the base of the river's great falls at Vergennes came the small American Lake Champlain squadron commanded by young Thomas Macdonough. As ice quickly sealed the lake, there was little doubt that come spring the British would move south from Canada, perhaps by both land and sea. President James Madison ordered that Macdonough build a much stronger lake force as fast as possible. Hill wrote: "His task seems a little less preposterous if 'nature's handmaid to industry,' the falls of the Otter, even then serving a surprising cluster of waterwheels, are taken into account. Charcoal and iron ore for the furnaces and forges were as plentiful as lumber for the up-and-down sawmills. Shipwrights were not, but Macdonough succeeded in securing one of the best, Noah Browne of New York, who agreed to launch at Vergennes a 24-gun ship in no less than 60 days. Since construction could not begin until early spring, and the ice would not leave the lake's Narrows perhaps until April, many supplies would have to come by land, despite all but impassable roads."

Supplies arrived by wagon as from far as Troy and Boston. Four-hundred militia came as well; they knew little about building ships but could swing axes, and timber for the new ships rolled in. As the weather warmed, the shipbuilding proceeded at a furious pace. Also, Vermont's governor Martin Chittenden responded to a call for more militia, finally sending 1,000 men. Many were dispatched to a point of land at the mouth of Otter Creek, where a battery was erected under the command of Lt. Stephen Cassin. On May 9, Capt. Daniel Pring headed south from the Richelieu with a British squadron that included the brig *Linnet* with 16 cannon, 13 galleys, and five sloops. Word of his approach spread along the lake's shores and artillerymen were rushed from Burlington. The Americans were full well ready at "Fort Cassin" when the British appeared on May 14. The British opened fire, shelling the fort for an hour-and-a-half, succeeding only in overturning one cannon and injuring two militiamen. Macdonough immediately dispatched some of his finished ships to the mouth of the creek, but well before they arrived, brisk fire from Fort Cassin drove off the British. Several American shots scored hits, and one British sailor reportedly was killed.

On May 26, Macdonough left his Vergennes shipyard and headed down Otter Creek with his flagship *Saratoga* and its 26 guns, the sloop *Preble* with nine cannon, the *Ticonderoga* with 16 guns, the sloops *President* and *Montgomery*, and six gunboats. Soon, four more gunboats joined the fleet and, in early August, the 120-foot-long *Eagle* sailed into the lake, having been built in 19 days. Macdonough was ready to do battle with the British who were also rushing boats to completion on the Richelieu River. In late May Macdonough sailed his new fleet into Plattsburgh Bay. The clash would come inside Cumberland Head at summer's end.

In the 1850s, a bearded farmer from North Elba in the Adirondacks often came to Vergennes on shopping trips. The Vergennes stores had more goods than any on the lake's New York side, since the railroad came up through Vermont. John Brown took the Adams ferry from Westport and became a rather familiar figure in town. Villagers who had dealings with him found him kindly, and very fond of children. And that was not surprising, since he sired 20 of his own by two wives. On one trip he bought a length of rope and legend persists in Vergennes that it was used in his hanging. Brown passed through Vergennes on his way to Harpers Ferry, headed south possessed by the idea of starting a slave uprising. Of course, his attack failed and no uprising resulted. Brown was severely wounded, captured, then tried, and

Vergennes railway station

hanged in Charles Town, Virginia (now West Virginia). His body came north by train accompanied by his widow, Mary Ann Brown. The casket, in a wooden box already damaged by souvenir hunters, was taken from the station at Vergennes and placed on a sleigh, for a light snow was down. Mrs. Brown rode on another sleigh, and the little procession advanced to the center of town. One contemporary account holds that a group of turkeys perked and clucked along behind. A crowd gathered as the procession stopped outside the Stevens House at the town's main intersection, and there were demands, to no avail, that the casket be opened. Then the sad little group proceeded down hill and across the Otter Creek Bridge, on its way to Arnold's Bay.

Touring Vergennes

The riverside park commands the best view of what is known locally as The Basin. The scene, looking across the historic waters to the Otter Creek Falls and the old buildings atop them, borders on spectacular. It was along the near shore, from the park to your left, that the American fleet was constructed. The two red brick buildings to your right, though looking ancient, were not standing during Macdonough's presence. But

The Basin, Vergennes

the large white house across the street, surrounded by a porch and much changed, witnessed the events of 1814. It was the home of Jahaziel Sherman, who ran the shipyard. Leaving the park, turn left and proceed to the top of the hill. Just past the summit are the grounds of the Northlands Job Corps Center. The second building on the left, the old stone structure, was built in 1828 as a United States arsenal and once held weapons that armed Vermont's Civil War regiments.

Return the way you came, pass the riverside park, then turn left up Battery Hill. The large old brick house at the top occupies the site of the artillery position built by Macdonough's men to greet any British intruders with cannon fire. Because the brave defenders of Fort Cassin did their jobs, the guns were never needed. Turn left on North Street and right on Green Street. Park on the left, and walk into Macdonough Park. The tree-shaded green in the center of town is a fine place for a picnic lunch, perhaps beside the impressive monument to the commodore. Walk to Main Street and stand at its intersection with Green Street. It is believed that Macdonough's office was located on the second floor of a building that stood on the southwest corner of the intersection. The building across the street, at the northwest corner, is the Stevens House where the procession taking John Brown's body home paused. Turn right and walk west along Main Street and note the stone block of stores on the south side where Brown once shopped. Continue along Main until you reach the Bixby Library, a graceful, domed structure with a fine collection relating to local history and friendly people always willing to answer questions.

Directions

Return to your car and turn left on Main Street, which is VT 22A. Go a bit less than a mile and on the right, set back from the road amid other buildings, is the old red railroad station where John Brown's body arrived. Continue on VT 22A until it reaches US 7, then turn north. Some 3 miles north of Vergennes and just beyond Ferrisburgh, on a low ridge to the east of US 7, stands the Rokeby Museum.

Chapter Thirteen

Rokeby to Burlington

ROKEBY MUSEUM

YOU MIGHT THINK that the home of a pacifist Quaker family would never be part of a military sites tour, but Rokeby must be visited. This remarkable place was a stop on the Underground Railroad, and as such was a part of the antislavery movement that preceded the Civil War.

Rokeby Museum

Open mid-May through mid-October, Thursday through Sunday; tours of the house begin at 11, 12:30, and 2. Admission fee.

Also, there simply is so much history here that to miss it is to render a tour of the Champlain Corridor incomplete. Built in the 1780s, Rokeby was for more than 150 years the home of the Robinson family. The Quaker Robinsons, strong abolitionists, in the 1830s opened their home to escaped slaves seeking freedom. The history of the Underground Railroad is difficult to trace because it was a secret operation carried out in defiance of the Fugitive Slave Laws. Though countless old houses throughout the northeastern United States claim to have been stops, Rokeby's authenticity is documented in letters sent to the Robinsons by slaves after having reached freedom in Canada. At Rokeby, the slaves not only were given shelter, but were paid to work, quite openly, in the 1,000-acre farm's fields. The museum displays a poster, produced by Rowland T. Robinson, for an antislavery meeting held in July 1843, that reads:

> There will be GREAT MEETINGS to examine the question of American Slavery, in Ferrisburgh Centre, on Monday and Tuesday the 17th & 18th instant . . . Frederick Douglass, the eloquent fugitive from slavery whose thrilling narration of his own history and sufferings while in bondage and powerful appeals for his oppressed brethren have accomplished so much in other states . . . will be present to address the convention.

A reception for Douglass was held at Rokeby, with local people meeting the guest of honor in the front parlor. That parlor, as is all of the house, is preserved as it was a very long time ago. The room looks about as it did the day Douglass visited, though the carpet has become frayed. Still, it is the one he walked upon. As the Civil War came, a young member of the Robinson family, William Stevens, against his parents' wishes enlisted in the Fourth Vermont Regiment. Willie Stevens was killed in the suicidal Union assault at Cold Harbor. His parents ever after displayed his picture on an upstairs wall and preserved his uniform, both of which may be seen today at Rokeby. Well after the war, the famed abolitionist William Lloyd Garrison wrote to his friend Rowland Robinson and recalled "the fiery old days" when both had agitated for human freedom. The letter, from one old man to another, closed: "It only remains for us to stand in our lot, and be dressed for the flight, and ready to be gone. If we should not meet again in the flesh, I have an unshaken faith that we shall be permitted to do so when 'clothed upon.'" Both Garrison and Robinson died the next year, in 1879.

Touring Rokeby

ROBINSON HOME

All visitors must first visit the Robinson House, and join a guided tour. The oldest part, the rear section, was built in the late 1780s, before Vermont became a state in 1791. Its kitchen with a walk-in fireplace is preserved. It is believed that escaped slaves who worked at Rokeby slept in the room above the kitchen. Go there and stand in a freedom shrine. The larger, front portion of the house was added in 1814, the year Commodore Macdonough fought the British.

Outbuildings

These include a combination granary and corn crib, the creamery where the Robinson family produced its famous "Rokeby butter," the three-holer outhouse, a smokehouse, and a slaughterhouse.

Sheep Dip

Follow a path south from the parking lot 100 yards to the sheep dip. The Robinsons built a stone dam on a stream south of the house, taking advantage of a natural rock outcropping. In the pool, sheep were washed before shearing. Rowland Evans Robinson described the process: "Huddled in a pen they are taken by the catcher as called for and carried to the washers, and passing from their hands, stagger water-logged and woe-begone, up the bank to rejoin their dripping comrades, and doubtless pass the hours while their fleeces are drying in mutual consolement over man's inhumanity to sheep."

Academy

A path beginning north of the house leads to the site of the Brick Academy, a two-story building with a cupola, that housed a school founded by Rowland T. Robinson in 1839. Both black and white children were educated there, before the Civil War. Rokeby hopes one day to rebuild the school that operated until 1846.

Farm Trail

Rokeby owns 90 acres of the original 1,000-acre Robinson Farm and a walking trail departing from the rear of the house winds through them. The walk begins along an abandoned farm road that tunnels through thick greenery. Signs along the way point to changing uses of the landscape, old stone walls, a stone well, the site of a very old apple orchard, and an old farm field still in use. At the spot most distant from the house is the walk's treasure, the Waterfall. In times of rain, particularly in the spring when the little stream has adequate flow, a small waterfall cascades down a sloping rock and into a secluded pool. This woodland glen is a place the Hudson River school painters would have loved. The brochure that guides your walk includes this quote from popular Vermont author Rowland Evans Robinson:

> "A day in the woods or by the streams is better for mind and body than one spent in idle gossip at the village store, and nine out of ten better for the pocket, though one come home without fin or feather to show for his day's outing."

One can imagine Robinson, sitting by the Waterfall on a day in spring, thinking deeply on the burning subject of his day, how to end the evil of slavery without bringing the nation to war. Much of the best is yet to come at Rokeby as plans are afoot to build an interpretive center that will tell the story of the Underground Railroad.

Directions

Continue north on US 7 and in 3.5 miles turn right on Mount Philo Road. The entrance to the Mount Philo State Park is ahead.

MOUNT PHILO

Mount Philo has no documented military history, though when one encounters the view from its summit, the thought immediately occurs that it must have been used as a lookout. The mount rises only 960 feet above sea level, a nubbin among Vermont summits. Yet because of its pre-

> Mount Philo State Park, which offers picnicking and camping, is open mid-May through mid-October. Admission fee.

cipitous rise from the Champlain Valley, its summit affords the best view in all of Vermont, surely one of the best in all the world.

Touring Mount Philo

Drive up the narrow and winding, though very safe, mile-long road to the top and park in the summit lot. Walk ahead along the short trail labeled SUMMIT SHELTER and see before you rock ledges topped by a cement platform surrounded by a railing. Hop up the rocks and encounter the stunning view to the south and west. Below you the lake stretches away from the harbor at Charlotte (you can see the Charlotte Ferry crossing the lake) far to the south. With binoculars, on a clear day, the Champlain Bridge and the plume from the Ticonderoga paper plant, not far from the fort, can be seen. There is no better view of what David Starbuck has called "The Great Warpath." One can easily imagine the armadas of Carleton and Burgoyne moving up the silver waters, beneath the formidable outline of the Adirondacks' High Peaks. Look to the east and the summit ridge of the Green Mountains is in view some 50 miles from Mount Abraham to the three distant clustered peaks of Pico, Killington, and Mendon.

Directions

From Mount Philo, return to US 7 and drive some 12 miles into Burlington. On entering the city, two-lane US 7 widens and becomes very busy. At the traffic circle, go a third of the way around, take Saint Paul Street, and in 0.75 mile turn left on King Street. Go three blocks and turn right on Battery Street. At the second light, turn left and drive onto the Burlington waterfront and park by the ECHO Center.

Chapter Fourteen

Burlington

ONE OF AMERICA'S LOVELIEST CITIES, situated on a broad harbor and commanding a view of the widest part of Lake Champlain, Burlington's military history is far less rich than Plattsburgh's, across the widest part of Champlain and to the north. Burlington, unlike Plattsburgh, was never seriously attacked, though on August 2, 1813, British ships shelled a battery erected on the high ground overlooking the harbor, now Battery Park. American gunners replied enthusiastically.

ECHO CENTER

Touring ECHO

The new ECHO at the Leahy Center for Lake Champlain on the Burlington waterfront must be visited. Named for Vermont's veteran U.S. Senator Patrick Leahy and his wife, Marcelle, but known as ECHO (for ecology, culture, history, and opportunity), the place opened in 2003 and visitors have streamed in ever since. ECHO's primary goal is to promote stewardship of the lake, to keep Lake Champlain

> The ECHO Center is open year-round 10–5, 10–8 on Thursday; closed Thanksgiving, Christmas Eve, and Christmas Day. Admission fee.

179

a vital, pollution-controlled waterway, and there is no better place to gain a quick understanding of what Lake Champlain is all about. Visitors are greeted in the lobby by a two-story waterfall that displays some of the region's fossils, up to 500 million years old. A video, *Forces of Nature*, explains the geology that shaped the Champlain basin. Watershed Way, a hands-on exhibit, allows children to manipulate miniature wetlands, dams, and boats to see their effects on the watershed. A replica of the *General Butler* shipwreck, which lies just beyond the Burlington harbor breakwater, allows children to climb and crawl about it. Tanks house Champlain life including giant sturgeon and catfish, tiny emerald shiners, frogs, turtles, and zebra mussels. The valley's weather is explained, as are the ways of life of the inhabitants. Though the exhibits seem mainly designed to attract and interest children, accompanying adults will find them fascinating and informative. One of the excellent features of the place is the deck on the second floor that overlooks the harbor and the wide lake. From it, you can see one of the best views along Champlain, and comfortable chairs invite you to take in the vista as long as you wish.

Directions
From ECHO, return to Battery Street, turn left, and go to the top of the hill. Turn left on North Avenue and go straight ahead into the parking lot for Battery Park.

BATTERY PARK

In 1812, with British forces assembling in southern Québec and the threat of an invasion on the rise, Colonel Isaac Clark of the 11th United States Infantry purchased 10 acres on the bluff overlooking Burlington Harbor for a military encampment. A brigade of four regi-

Note: A Lake Champlain Navy Memorial will soon be completed at Hoehl Park, on the north side of ECHO. Featuring a statue of a modern-day sailor looking toward the lake, plans are to offer information on the lake's naval history at the memorial.

Battery Park, Burlington

ments passed the winter there. The following summer a fortification was erected along the blufftop, made of packed sod, with embrasures for 13 cannon. By July 1813, 3,000 men were camped on what became known as The Battery. Large wooden barracks were erected for the men and smaller cottages for the officers. On July 30, Gen. Wade Hampton, grandfather of the famed Confederate cavalryman of the same name, arrived to take command. By the beginning of August, Hampton's force consisted of more than 4,000 men, though some 500 reportedly were sick.

Battery Park is a public park and is always open. No admission fee.

As Hampton reached Burlington, the British were on the move south. A land force raided Plattsburgh on July 31, and on Monday, August 2, the British ships *Broke* and *Shannon* appeared off Burlington Harbor. Anchored under the battery were several of Macdonough's ships, though only one sloop and two small gunboats were fit for duty. At 2:30 that afternoon the British ships approached with the suspected intent of destroying three storehouses on the wharf. American soldiers stood by their guns on the high-sited Battery. The British had just opened fire when, about a mile-and-a-half out, a response came immediately from the Battery's artillery, from Macdonough's ships, and from a scow armed with two 12-pounders. The brisk exchange lasted 20 minutes, until the attackers drew off to the south. The British were pursued briefly by some of Macdonough's ships, which turned back believing that other British vessels might be lying in wait. Several houses along the waterfront had been hit by British shells.

During the Battle of Plattsburgh, the sounds of war were clearly heard 25 miles away by the people of Burlington, gathered on the waterfront. That night, the city's bells were rung in celebration and victory salutes were fired by the big guns along The Battery. The victorious American commanders Macdonough and General Macomb arrived in Burlington 12 days after the battle and were guests of honor at a parade, banquet, and ball. On October 12, 1814, Macdonough sailed his ship *Saratoga* and the captured *Confiance* past Burlington on their way to Whitehall and retirement. Cannon on The Battery saluted them as they passed just outside the harbor.

Touring Battery Park

The view from Battery Park has, rightfully, been called one of the finest in North America. From this elevated vantage point with Burlington Harbor directly below, one looks across the widest part of Lake Champlain to the New York shore and the Adirondack Mountains. Nine-acre Battery Park is said to encompass the area of the parade ground at the old War of 1812 encampment. Two markers recall the brief cannon exchange between the Battery and British ships. The wall and walk along the bluff run along the location of the old 13-embrasure battery, which long ago disappeared. Recent archaeological explorations in neighborhoods near the park have uncovered several skeletons, believed to have been American soldiers who died during their War of 1812 service. Also in the park is a monument to one of Vermont's important Civil War figures, Brig.-Gen. William Wells. His statue is a copy of one that stands at the base of Big Round Top, at Gettysburg. Wells rose from the rank of private to command the First Vermont Cavalry Regiment. He was a leader of the cavalry charge launched after Pickett's Charge was repulsed on July 3, 1863.

Directions

From the parking lot turn left, north, on North Avenue, and in just under 1.5 miles turn right on VT 127. Make a quick left at the ETHAN ALLEN HOMESTEAD sign.

ETHAN ALLEN HOMESTEAD

In the words of historian Ralph Nading Hill: "In 1787 Ethan moved north to Burlington with his second wife and their children (his first wife had died) and settled in a modest house on the Onion near the lake, there to farm his lands in the Inter-

The homestead is open daily 9–5, May through October, and Saturday in the winter. Admission fee.

vale and to write his free-thinking book on religion, *Reason the Only Oracle of Man.*" The hero of Ticonderoga was 50 and his adventures were behind him. Only memory now were his rabble-rousing along the New York border, his fights with claimants to the lands that would become

Ethan Allen Homestead

the State of Vermont, his attack on the once-mighty fort at Ticonderoga, and his undermanned, probably foolish, advance on Montréal. Also in the past were his years in a British prison, his triumphant return, and the strange negotiations with the British in 1780, apparently on the possibility of Vermont becoming a part of the British Empire. The so-called Haldimand negotiations left some pondering whether there was a bit of the traitor in Ethan Allen, though he may well have been attempting to pressure Congress to admit Vermont as its 14th state.

But now he had come to a farmhouse overlooking the Winooski (or Onion) River, a pleasant house on the fertile ground of Burlington's Intervale, the 800 acre floodplain near the Winooski's mouth. He took up residence in the two-story home with his wife, Fanny, their three children, three children by his first marriage, two farmhands, and a maid. They all lived under the same roof, in a house with a sizeable parlor, a common room, and a smaller room where Allen wrote. Also, the large attic was available for storage, and perhaps for sleeping in the warmer months. But it was too cold to inhabit in the winter, making for a crowded condition downstairs.

Perhaps this was the place of Allen's dreams, a fine little home in an idyllic setting among fertile farm fields. But alas, he was to enjoy but two years in this pleasant place. Setting off up the river, then out onto Lake Champlain, at the beginning of February 1789, Allen and a servant were bound across the frozen lake to fetch a load of hay from Ebenezer Allen at his farm on Grand Isle. Allen stayed the night, and perhaps a good time was had by all. Was the flowing bowl passed? Next morning Allen and his servant began the return journey. All went well until the sleigh approached the mouth of the Winooski, where Ethan remarked, "It seems as if the trees are very thick here." Then he began to struggle, obviously very ill, the servant making every effort to keep him from falling from the sleigh. Finally arriving at the house, a physician was summoned who resorted to a common medical practice of the day. Ethan was bled. Despite, or because of, that treatment, he was dead in just a few hours.

Today, in the lobby of the Visitors Center are several quotations concerning the remarkable man who lived the last two years of his life here. Among them:

One day, hunting, Allen came upon some deer, killed one and hung his hat on it to keep the ravens away. Then he killed another, and hung his jacket on it. On the next, his breeches. Finally he killed another deer, and with its skin around him, went to camp.—Brother Ira Allen, 1772

Though born in New England, he exhibited no trace of her character. He was frank, bluff, companionable as a Pagan, convivial, a Roman, hearty as a harvest. His spirit was essentially western, and herein is his peculiar Americanism; for the Western spirit is, or will be (for no other is, or can be) the true American one.—Herman Melville, 1855

And the words of Ethan himself are displayed:

In a fit of anger I twisted off a nail with my teeth . . . I heard one say . . . damn him, can he eat iron?

While imprisoned on a British ship:

The Gods of the Hills are not the Gods of the Valleys.

Those last words, spoken in 1770 during the border disputes with New York, have echoed down the years as perhaps the best of all fighting words a Vermonter ever uttered, also a testament to the state's, and its people's, uniqueness. They speak well of Ethan's love of the land that two years after his death became the 14th state of the United States of America.

Touring the Homestead

The Visitors Center, with a gift shop, is located in a refurbished barn and offers displays on Allen, including artifacts dug around the home, and a multimedia presentation on his life. Tours are conducted hourly to the house, located about 100 yards behind the barn. For years, some controversy existed concerning whether the house was, indeed, the last home of Allen. But recent investigations have all but sealed the certainty that the little structure overlooking the Winooski is Ethan's last abode.

Gardens have been re-created near the house such as Ethan's wife, Fannie, would have tended to supply her kitchen. The house, much used and lived in since Ethan's days, has been extensively restored and a sizeable 19th-century addition has been stripped away. The house now appears as it must have at the time of the Allen occupation. But little of the original structure remains, save for the supporting posts and the roof. Be sure to look up the stairs and see the wide roof boards that sheltered the old rebel in his last days. One has a feeling that Allen would readily recognize, and perhaps feel at home, in the old place. Indeed, those who work here often sense a presence, especially late in the day, and some speak of a strange play of shadows.

Tours include much information on the way people lived in the late 1700s, and many period pieces of furniture, tools, and utensils furnish the house. The tour also leads to an overlook on the front lawn with a view along the Winooski. Surely it was here, coming up the bank from the river to the front door behind you, that the dying Ethan was brought on that sad day in 1789.

The grounds of the homestead contain picnic areas, walking, and ski trails. Many people rent the picnic shelter for various gatherings.

Directions

From the parking lot, return to VT 127, and turn left, or north. VT 127 winds along the bank of the Winooski, following the route, in reverse, of Ethan's last ride along the frozen river. In a little less than 3 miles the highway crosses the river and just under 5 miles farther be sure to turn right on Lake Shore Drive at the T-intersection to stay on VT 127 north. One mile beyond, turn left on Lakeshore Drive, thus leaving VT 127, and drive along the pleasant shore of Malletts Bay. In just under 3 miles stop and turn sharp left on US 7 north. In another 3 miles turn left and go north on I-89 at the Colchester interchange, bound for St. Albans. Follow I-89 north for 16.5 miles to Exit 19, the St. Albans exit. Proceed 1 mile to US 7 and turn north. You are now on St. Albans's Main Street. Arriving at the corner of the city green, Taylor Park, turn right and then take a quick left on Church Street along the east side of the park. The second building is the St. Albans Historical Society Museum. Park in the rear.

Chapter Fifteen

St. Albans and the Raid

OF ALL THE PLACES where Civil War fighting erupted, St. Albans in far northern Vermont may be the most implausible. In the autumn of 1864, the war was going full tilt on three major fronts, far from Vermont, the closest being more than 500 miles from the railroad community of St. Albans. Ulysses Grant had Petersburg under siege threatening the Confederate capital of Richmond. In the Shenandoah Valley, Phil Sheridan had smashed a Confederate army under Jubal Early at Winchester and Fisher's Hill and Sheridan's Army of the Valley had gone into camp behind meandering Cedar Creek. Way south, William Tecumseh Sherman had captured Atlanta. In thriving St. Albans, certainly everyone seemed a long way from danger.

Still, in addressing the Vermont Legislature on October 12, 1864, Governor John Gregory Smith, a St. Albans resident, had raised concern about security along the Canadian border. That message likely came to the attention of a stranger, claiming to be a theology student, who appeared in St. Albans in early October. Bennett Young, a handsome young man perhaps betraying the slightest hint of a southern accent, spent much of the next few days riding about the colorful countryside, and reading a Bible in his hotel lobby. And there were other strangers in town, though nobody paid much attention, young men who had taken rooms at three local hostelries. One even told a desk clerk his name was Jefferson Davis. No matter, this was a railroad place with unfamiliar people always coming and going.

Then, on October 19, the theology student donned a gray uniform, revealing himself to be an officer in the Confederate army, and suddenly some 20 Rebels were on Main Street, entering the town's three banks and demanding all the money. "Not a word," said a raider, "we are Confederate soldiers, have come to take your town, have a large force. We shall take your money, and if you resist, will blow your brains out. We are going to do what Sheridan has been doing in the Shenandoah Valley."

Stunned townspeople were herded into Taylor Park where armed men kept them under close watch. Local bankers proved uncooperative, but still the Confederates filled sacks with 208,000 Vermont dollars. Some local people hastened home to get their guns and began firing at the Confederates, severely wounding one raider. Mounting stolen horses, the raiders gathered on Main Street and started north, throwing bottles of "Greek fire" at buildings along the way, hoping to burn Yankee St. Albans to the ground. The grenades fizzled, giving off much smoke but little flame. One civilian, a New Hampshire man, Elinus Morrison, overseeing construction of a new hotel, was mortally wounded along the sidewalk.

A posse was quickly organized and went pounding off in hot pursuit just 20 minutes behind the raiders. A few miles beyond town, on the Sheldon Road, the raiders came on a Vermonter riding a fine horse. At gunpoint, the man was relieved of his mount and given an exhausted horse. When the posse came in sight, recognizing one of the stolen horses, it opened fire on the poor man. He saved his life only by running into an alder swamp. The raiders galloped on to Sheldon Springs, where another bank they hoped to rob had closed for the day. On reaching the village of Sheldon, they tried to burn a covered bridge and halt the posse. But they failed, and quickly galloped across the smoking structure, as did the posse a short while later. The raiders crossed the swift Missisquoi River at Enosburg Falls, then divided into small parties and made their way to the border over a variety of routes. They all reached Canada safely, though the posse continued its pursuit, some members even crossing the international boundary. Young and several of his followers were seized next morning on Canadian soil. But Canadian authorities intervened, taking 14 Confederates to Montréal to stand trial. A hanging likely awaited the bank robbers back in Vermont, but a Canadian magistrate ordered that the men not be ex-

tradited. Thus Young and his band got away with their crime, and
$208,000. Later, some $80,000 was returned to St. Albans by the
Canadian government, too late to save two of the plundered banks,
which failed because of the cash losses. Five days after the raid, a
Burlington paper reported on St. Albans:

> The excitement in the borough has by no means subsided. Revolvers
> are the most saleable articles of hardware, and rumors of all sorts of
> coming horrors keep prudent people on the alert and nervous persons
> in a state of chronic perspiration. The rumors of to-day are that Platts-
> burgh was invaded yesterday and the banks robbed by a party of
> raiders, and that authentic advices have been received by Governor
> Smith that two thousand armed and organized rebels in Canada are
> about to invade St. Albans and complete the devastation which the
> rebels left unfinished.

But no more Confederates appeared, and the northernmost land
action of the Civil War was history. It should be noted that as Young
and his men fled St. Albans, some 600 miles to the south, in the
Shenandoah Valley, Phil Sheridan was winning a major victory at
Cedar Creek, a victory that would assure Abraham Lincoln of reelec-
tion and the pursuit of the Union war effort to total victory.

ST. ALBANS HISTORICAL SOCIETY

The society is housed in the former St. Albans
Grammar School, built in 1862. The top floor is
an elegant old auditorium where abolitionists
once spoke and young men were recruited to
serve in Vermont Civil War units. At the time of

Open 1–4, June 1 through
September 30, Monday
through Friday. Admission
fee.

the raid, the building was filled with school children, with most on the
top floor. When word of the raid reached the school, the children were
hastened below, but caught glimpses of the action in Taylor Park and
along Main Street through stairway windows as they descended.

A first-floor room contains dioramas of the Champlain Valley,
and of St. Albans at the time of the raid. Push a button and hear an

interesting description of the raid, decidedly Yankee, the narrator re-
ferring to the raiders as a "trigger-happy pack of Confederates." On the
wall are framed several Yankee dollars stolen by the raiders, reward
posters, photos of Bennett Young and some of his men. Also visit the
museum's military room displaying items from many of the nation's
wars, including Gen. George Stannard's saddle. Stannard commanded
the Second Vermont Brigade that broke the right flank of Pickett's
Charge at Gettysburg.

Touring the City

Downtown St. Albans is an attractive and compact community, and
one may either walk or drive to sites associated with the raid. On
emerging from the museum, note that all buildings along this east side
of the park witnessed the raid. Walk into Taylor Park, recalling that the
raiders kept many townspeople under guard here. It is also worth
noting that a year after the Civil War, Gen. George Meade, the victor
at Gettysburg, came to St. Albans to keep an eye on a group of Irish
Fenians intent on invading Canada. Meade's men camped in the park.

From the museum, return to Church Street and turn right. Go to
the corner of Bank Street and turn left. At Main Street, turn left and
go to the traffic light, then turn right onto Lake Street. At the first intersection, the brick-and-clapboard building on the left, with porches,
was the St. Albans House, a hotel where some of the raiders stayed.
Pass through the intersection and the large brick building on the right
is the St. Albans railway station, which stands on the site of the old station where the raiders arrived. The long red building beyond it, once a
railroad facility, stood in 1864. Return up Lake Street and note the
brick building on the northwest corner of Lake and Main, the much-
renovated America House, where Bennett Young and other raiders
stayed and where the wounded Elinus Morrison died. Look to the
right, beyond the corner of Taylor Park, to an auto dealership where
one of the robbed banks once stood. Turn north along Main Street and
note the Franklin County Bank on the left, built on the site of another
robbed bank. Farther north along Main at the corner of Kingman
Street, a large three-story brick structure stands on the site of the third

bank. A bit north along Main Street is City Hall, built on the site of the hotel where Young assembled his men the day of the raid. On the west side of Main is a white two-story brick building with a large modern display window. The wounded Morrison was taken to this building, before being carried to his room in the America House. Before leaving St. Albans, the visitor might want to stop at Greenwood Cemetery, a half mile south of Taylor Park on Main Street. Several people who figured in the story of the raid lie there, including Capt. George Conger, who organized and led the posse, and Governor Smith. Near the entrance is a stone that vividly records a family's anger at the loss of a son to the Civil War. Joseph Brainerd, a local abolitionist, had a memorial stone erected in the family plot on learning of his son's death in the Confederate prison at Andersonville. The body never came home and lies in the national cemetery at Andersonville. On the stone is carved:

> JOSEPH PARTRIDGE BRAINERD. SON OF JOSEPH AND HIS WIFE FANNY PARTRIDGE. A CONSCIENTIOUS FAITHFUL BRAVE UNION SOLDIER. WAS BORN ON THE 27TH DAY OF JUNE 1840. GRADUATED FROM THE UNIVERSITY OF VERMONT IN AUGUST 1862. ENLISTED INTO COMPANY L OF THE VERMONT CAVALRY WAS WOUNDED AND TAKEN PRISONER BY THE REBELS IN THE WILDERNESS MAY 5 1864 WAS SENT TO ANDERSONVILLE PRISON PEN IN GEORGIA WHERE HE DIED ON THE 11TH DAY OF SEPTEMBER 1864 ENTIRELY AND WHOLLY NEGLECTED BY PRESIDENT LINCOLN AND MURDERED WITH IMPUNITY BY THE REBELS, WITH THOUSANDS OF OUR LOYAL SOLDIERS BY STARVATION PRIVATION EXPOSURE AND ABUSE.

Following the Raiders

Go north on Main Street, along which many of the houses were witnesses to the 1864 events, to follow the raiders' escape route. Turn right on VT 105 where the road divides. Six miles from the beginning of VT 105, note a thickly forested swampy area on the left. This may be where the St. Albans man unluckily riding a stolen horse fled into the woods to save his life. In another 2.5 miles you will pass Sheldon Springs, where the raiders failed to rob the bank. In 1 mile, bear right where a sign points to Sheldon, and continue 2 miles to the center of the village. Turn sharp left and cross a cement bridge, built on the site

America House, where some of the Confederate raiders stayed in St. Albans, Vermont.

of the covered bridge the raiders tried to burn. Cross the bridge and continue following the Confederates' escape, some 7 miles through the hills along the south side of the Missisquoi. Reaching a point where the road seems about to end, turn left and go up over the hill. At the top, look down on Enosburg. Night had come by the time the raiders reached this point. Surely, looking down on the lights of the town, they wondered whether word of their deeds had reached the citizenry and a fiery reception might await them. Continue to Enosburg Falls, crossing the Missisquoi on a modern bridge. Beside it is a now-closed arched cement bridge that replaced the covered bridge used by the raiders. North of Enosburg Falls, after passing quietly through the village, the raiders split up and their routes are impossible to follow.

Directions
In Enosburg, take VT 105 west and return to St. Albans. Just north of the city, pick up I-89 south to Exit 16 and take US 2 west. Passing through marshes, and just before reaching the lakeshore and the long causeway connecting the mainland with Grand Isle, turn into the boat access area on the left.

Chapter Sixteen

Plattsburgh and Its Battles

SANDBAR

This is Sandbar, a place commanding a good view across part of Lake Champlain to Grand Isle and the Adirondack Mountains beyond. The pointed peak is Whiteface Mountain, at Lake Placid near where John Brown lived. In the fall of 1812 there was no causeway at Sandbar, but the lake was so shallow that horses could be waded to Grand Isle. Here many Vermont volunteers made the first leg of their lake crossing on their way to fight in the Battle of Plattsburgh.

Directions

From Sandbar, continue west on US 2 following signs for the ferry to Plattsburgh. Boats run throughout the year from 6 AM to 11 PM, and the crossing takes about 15 minutes. From the ferry, looking directly ahead, the big old Hotel Champlain, now Clinton Community College, stands on a bluff on the New York shore. Well out in the bay, but appearing to be just in front of the old hotel, is little Crab Island. South of the hotel, the long, low, dark profile of Valcour Island is visible. Approaching the ferry slip and crossing the British fleet's course in 1814, recall that the untested American seamen could see the fearsome sight of tall British masts approaching beyond Cumberland Head, where you are about to land.

PLATTSBURGH

On a day in December 1812, Lieut. Thomas Macdonough took his bride, Lucy Ann Shaler Macdonough, on a 20-mile sleigh ride from Burlington across frozen Lake Champlain to Plattsburgh. There they called at the home of Peter Sailly, collector of customs, and apparently the young couple met Henry and Betsy DeLord. Henceforth, when the Macdonoughs visited Plattsburgh, they usually called at the home of Henry and Betsy DeLord that overlooks the mouth of the Saranac River and Plattsburgh Bay (now known as the Kent Museum, or Kent-DeLord House). Little did the Macdonoughs know that, in less than two years, the DeLord house would be in British hands. And offshore, in the very waters the Macdonoughs could see from the DeLord windows, Thomas Macdonough would fight a British fleet in a bloody battle that would help to decide the War of 1812.

Certainly Macdonough, a well-trained American officer, was well aware of his country's brief naval history and of its naval tactics. Surely he knew how Benedict Arnold had positioned his little fleet behind Valcour Island in 1776 to give battle. Macdonough must have taken a hard look at Valcour in his travels along the lake. Indeed, he seems to have employed the lessons of Valcour in his own battle plan in 1814. Arnold, who by 1814 was the most infamous of American traitors, was in 1776 a true American hero. In the fall of that year he masted his little Skenesborough-built Lake Champlain fleet at Mount Independence, then sailed north to Crown Point. On August 24 he moved north with nine ships and boats carrying 55 cannon, 78 swivel guns, and 395 men. Running into bad weather, he and his fleet were unable to reach the northern section of the lake until September 6, finally anchoring near Isle La Motte. There they were ambushed by Algonquins who killed three of Arnold's men.

On September 23 Arnold received reinforcements, bringing his

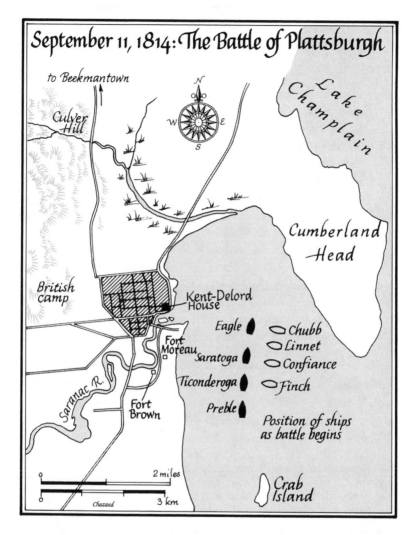

September 11, 1814: The Battle of Plattsburgh

to Beekmantown

Culver Hill

Lake Champlain

Cumberland Head

British camp

Kent-Delord House

Eagle

Chubb

Linnet

Confiance

Fort Moreau

Saratoga

Ticonderoga

Finch

Saranac R.

Fort Brown

Preble

Position of ships as battle begins

2 miles

3 km

Chazaud

Crab Island

fleet to 15 vessels, and he pulled in behind Valcour Island, which lies just off the New York shore south of Plattsburgh. There in the mile-wide channel between island and mainland he waited, with both flanks well protected, for the much larger British fleet. On October 12 the British, under Sir Guy Carleton, came south out of the Richelieu before a strong north wind. Arriving at the southern tip of Valcour and spotting the Americans, the British advance on Arnold's line was made difficult by the need to turn north against the wind. When the fighting opened, Arnold's flagship, the *Royal Savage*, was quickly hit with several cannon shots and ran aground on Valcour. Transferring with his flag to the *Congress*, Arnold described the battle:

> The schooner (*Royal Savage*), by some bad management, fell to leeward and was first attacked; one of her masts was wounded, and her rigging shot away. The captain thought prudent to run her on the point of Valcour where all the men were saved. They boarded her, and at night set fire to her. At half-past twelve, the engagement became general and very warm. Some of the enemy's ships and all her gondolas beat and rowed up within musket-shot of us. They continued a very hot fire with round and grapeshot until five o'clock, when they thought proper to retire to about six or seven hundred yards distance, and continued to fire until dark. The *Congress* and *Washington* have suffered greatly; the latter lost her first lieutenant killed, captain and master wounded. The *New York* lost all her officers, except the captain. The *Philadelphia* was hulled in so many places that she sunk in about one hour after the engagement was over. The whole killed and wounded amounts to about sixty.

Baron von Riedesel was on a British ship, and he spoke of "a tremendous cannonade" on both sides. Arnold, the experienced seaman, took to pointing cannon himself. And from Valcour, Indians fighting with the British peppered the American vessels, though apparently with little effect. As darkness descended on the bloody scene, the British withdrew to the mouth of the channel, to block any escape attempt, waiting to finish the Americans the next morning. That night, a fog descended on the channel and in the darkness and mists, Arnold started his battered fleet south, silently and single file along the New York shore, finding just enough room to slip his boats undetected past the west end of the British line. Dawn and the lifting fog displayed to an infuriated Carleton the American fleet with a big head start south. The commander ordered an immediate pursuit. Arnold was forced to sink two leaking gunboats near Schuyler Island. A fierce battle erupted near Split Rock and the battered *Lee* had to be run ashore and the shot-up ships, the *Washington* and the *New Jersey*, surrendered.

Arnold was forced to put in at the Ferris House, on what would ever after be known as Arnold's Bay, and flee overland to safety. At the end of the two-day running battle, only the schooner *Revenge*, the sloop *Enterprise*, the galley *Trumbull*, and one gunboat made it safely to Crown Point.

Certainly Thomas Macdonough recalled that story of 1776 as nearly four decades later, in the northern lake, he awaited another British naval force. In the late summer of 1814, it was well known that the British were coming again. They were moving south by land and water, on land with some 10,000 troops, many of them veterans of the Napoleonic Wars. On the lake they came with a fleet outgunning and outmanning Macdonough's little navy and including one monster vessel, the *Confiance*. Macdonough, much like Arnold, forced the British to attack upwind, not by anchoring behind Valcour Island, but by taking position in Plattsburgh Bay, behind Cumberland Head.

The British army under Lt. Gen. Sir George Prevost marched toward Plattsburgh early the morning of September 6. North of Beekmantown, Prevost divided his force into two columns—one advancing on the Shore Road, the other coming south on the inland Beekmantown Road. Both columns soon encountered resistance from 400 Americans staging a brief fight at Culver Hill on the Beekmantown Road and 150 troops taking shots at the King's fighters on the Shore Road. Casualties were suffered in both fights as the Americans withdrew. On the Shore Road, as the British approached Plattsburgh, they came under fire from some of Macdonough's ships sent close to shore. But British cannon soon drove the American ships out of range. Continuing south on the Shore Road, that British advance came under musket fire at Reverend Halsey's Farm (now Halsey's Corners) where several soldiers fell.

Prevost, intent on finding a route of attack around the American left flank, sent a column to the west that struck both the Saranac River and an American guard at Waite's Mill. After a brief firefight, the British withdrew. By the time the day ended, the Americans had all crossed the Saranac River to the protection of three partially constructed forts and two blockhouses, all on the river's south bank.

Facing the mighty British force were less than 4,000 men, including 2,500 Vermont militia who had crossed the lake to bolster the 1,500 regular soldiers and New York militia already at Plattsburgh. Skirmishing continued the next four days, with the British pounding the village and the American positions with both cannon and rocket fire. One night a heroic American raiding party quietly crossed the Saranac River from Fort Brown and disrupted the building of a British battery.

Prevost waited to attack until British ships came in view. As previously planned, his majesty's ships arrived on the morning of September 11, and fighting promptly began on the shore. On the lake, with the sighting of the British ships' masts, there was a silent moment of prayer aboard Macdonough's flagship the *Saratoga*. Anchored from northeast to southwest across the mouth of Cumberland Bay, the American ships the *Preble*, *Ticonderoga*, *Eagle*, and *Saratoga* awaited the big *Confiance* and her sister ships, the *Finch*, *Chubb*, and the *Linnet*. The British approach was hampered by the need to tack against the north wind, but on they came, swinging majestically into line of battle as the American gunners stood their posts. A shot from the American *Eagle* opened the battle. The *Linnet* quickly loosed a broadside at the *Saratoga*, one shot smashing open the cage of the crew's pet gamecock. The startled bird flapped up into the rigging, where it stayed for the rest of the battle. The *Saratoga* and the *Confiance* engaged, and the decks of both ships were quickly bloodied. The exchanges were heavy and repeated, with both ships taking telling hits. Capt. George Downie, of the *Confiance*, was killed within the battle's first 15 minutes.

"The firing was terrific, fairly shaking the ground," recalled a man who saw the battle from the shore, "and so rapid that it seemed to be one continuous roar, intermingled with the spiteful flashing from the mouths of guns, and dense clouds of smoke soon hung over the two fleets."

Macdonough was knocked briefly unconscious by falling rigging, and later he was felled by a man's severed head. But the *Confiance*, presented with a fresh broadside after taking several telling hits, surrendered at 11 AM. The *Saratoga* then went after the crippled *Linnet*, which soon surrendered. To the south of the line, the British ship *Finch*, under heavy fire from the *Ticonderoga*, ran aground on the shoals off Crab Island. Earlier, the British *Chubb*, smashed by the *Eagle*'s cannon, drifted out of action. The British had been battered and less than 150 minutes after the first shot was fired, it was all over as they signaled surrender. A Vermonter who witnessed the battle, and then rowed out to the battered *Saratoga*, related:

> "When we climbed up on the deck we found it slippery with blood and almost covered with the wounded and the dead. We saw a man walking quickly back and forth on the quarterdeck, his cap pulled down over his eyes and his face and hands almost black with powder and smoke. Upon asking who the man was the sailor replied, 'That's Commodore Macdonough.'"

> "They came under convoy guard directly from the flagship *Confiance*, and as they stepped on the deck of the *Saratoga* they met Commodore Macdonough, who kindly bowed to them," said a man who saw the surrender, "while they, holding their caps in their left hands and their swords, by the blades, in their right, advanced toward him and, bowing, presented their weapons. The Commodore bowed and said, 'Gentlemen, return your swords into your scabbards and wear them. You are worthy of them. And having obeyed the order, arm in arm, with their swords by their sides, they walked the decks of their conqueror." The decks had, indeed, run red with blood. The Americans suffered 52 killed and 58 wounded, the British, 54 killed and 116 wounded.

On land, the morning of September 11, particularly around the Kent-DeLord House where Macdonough had once been a guest, British cannon and rockets opened on the Americans across the Saranac. The fire was enthusiastically returned. The British attempted to ford the river in the heart of town, along Bridge Street, but Americans fighting from behind a breastwork made from rails of the torn up bridge turned them back. Meanwhile, Americans working cannon in Fort Brown just to the south on a bluff above the Saranac took and received heavy fire. But the action in and around the village was but a feint as 4,000 British troops, having crossed the Saranac at Fredenburgh Falls well west of the village, moved up onto the sand plains above the river. The American commander, Alexander Macomb, had anticipated the British end run, and he was ready when the redcoats appeared. Amid scrub pines the British encountered fire from New York militia. As the British came on, the New Yorkers gave way until Vermonters, waiting in ambush with American regulars, opened up.

The spirited battle was just beginning to rage when the British command heard cheering from the American lines. Word soon reached them, too, of the loss of their big ship, the *Confiance*. Prevost, sensing doom on the bay, ordered a withdrawal. So the British pulled back across the Saranac, taking casualties as they did. Soon Prevost was notified of the fleet's surrender and well before nightfall all his troops were back in their pre-attack positions. Before morning, the entire British army was tramping toward Canada. Prevost knew that without control of the lake, his invading force could not be supplied. Certainly, Burgoyne's fate a generation before haunted his thinking.

In Plattsburgh, the local newspaper reported that "from September 6 until evening on the 11th, scarcely a building escaped injury . . . nine houses, thirteen stores, the courthouse and jail were burned." At the Kent-DeLord House, the DeLord family hurried into their back yard and dug up silver they had buried as the British advanced.

From the battered ships, British and American wounded were taken to Crab Island for treatment in the American hospital there. The dead seamen were buried on the island in a common mass grave. Ashore, dead British and American officers were interred in the village cemetery, with full honors.

The Battle of Plattsburgh had been the decisive engagement of the War of 1812. On Christmas Eve, 1814, the conflict ended with the signing of the Treaty of Ghent, and with America's borders secure. Macdonough and Macomb became American heroes, honors pouring in from near and far. Among them was the gift, to Macdonough, from the people of Vermont, of a farm overlooking Plattsburgh Bay. Though the commodore never made use of it, the land has remained in the Macdonough family.

Directions

From the Plattsburgh Ferry, turn left toward Plattsburgh; in a mile you'll see an old marker on the right at the Macdonough farm. A third of a mile farther, pull into a small plaza on the right where an interpretive sign facing Plattsburgh Bay and the scene of the naval battle briefly describes the fight. Continue 2.5 miles to the intersection of US 9. Turn left and proceed south along US 9 for a mile, turning left onto

The Macdonough Monument, Plattsburgh, New York

Cumberland Avenue at a Heritage Trail sign. You soon come to a monument to Samuel Champlain, which overlooks the mouth of the Saranac River. Across the street is the Kent-DeLord House, in British hands during the battle. Continue past the house and you quickly reach City Hall Place. On the left is the soaring, eagle-topped monument to Macdonough's victory, with the names of his ships on each side. The monument, with a long, winding stairway to an observation deck, is

Samuel de Champlain Monument

seldom open. Proceed past domed and columned City Hall and look for signs for US 9 south. Take that route and soon you see the Plattsburgh military base on your left. Proceed to the roundabout, go two-thirds of the way around, and enter the old military base on Vermont Avenue. Turn in to the new Interpretive Center at your first right.

Battle of Plattsburgh Interpretive Center

Opened in September 2004, the center features a diorama of both the land and naval battles of 1814. This is the place to begin your tour of Plattsburgh. This lakeside city can be confusing, an old place with many streets whose courses are affected by the river winding through it. Obtain a map of the city at the Interpretive Center to guide in seeking key battle sites. In touring Plattsburgh, we deviate from our usual tour format of history and directions because of the complexity of the city and battle sites. Again, obtain a map.

The Interpretive Center is open 10–2, Tuesday through Saturday, year-round.

The following places must be seen, though they are but a partial list of the historic sites in Plattsburgh:

PLATTSBURGH MILITARY BASE

The Interpretive Center is located in the base's former museum. The base dates to the War of 1812 and was an active military post (at times serving the army, navy, and air force) into the 1990s. Be sure and see the old barracks, built in 1838, where local historians insist Ulysses Grant was once briefly stationed. Also, obtain directions at the center to the overlooks on the far side of the base that provide a fine view of Crab Island and the area of the naval battle. And drive about the base, being sure to swing around The Oval, the old parade ground. At its north end is the site of Fort Moreau, largest of the three forts that saw action in 1814. Near the south end of the base is the Post Cemetery, where rest 136 unknown soldiers from the Battle of Plattsburgh. A monument honors them.

Old barracks, Plattsburgh

FORT BROWN

Walk to Fort Brown from the Interpretive Center because there is no parking by the fort. The fort lies on the far side of US 9, about five-minutes distance. The large earthen fort both gave and took fire before and during the Battle of Plattsburgh, and from it an American raiding party went out in the night to attack the British on the far bank of the Saranac.

Fort Brown historic marker

Kent-DeLord House

Located on Cumberland Avenue, the house was in British hands during the battle and cannon located nearby fired on the Americans across the river. The house, built in 1797 and subsequently enlarged, is beautifully restored, with period furniture and art. A sideboard in the front hall is said to have been broken into by the British. Indeed, one door does not match and it probably replaced the one smashed by the invaders. But the great treasure of the house is a small portrait of Macdonough given to the DeLords by the commodore. The look in his eyes is of defiance. The house also has a Civil War exhibit that includes a Medal of Honor awarded to Chaplain Francis Hall of the 16th New York Regiment for gallantry in the 1863 Battle of Salem Church, Virginia.

The Kent-DeLord House

CITY HALL

Located at City Hall Place, this graceful domed building's lobby is devoted to an exhibit on the Battle of Plattsburgh, which includes an anchor from the *Confiance*, the 146-foot-long, British ship with at least 36 guns. Three of the big ship's huge anchors were shot

Open Monday through Friday, 8–4. Free admission.

away during the battle, making it nearly helpless in the face of heavy American fire. The lobby also contains murals depicting the battle, along with other scenes of Plattsburgh history.

BRIDGE STREET BRIDGE

Located on Bridge Street in downtown Plattsburgh and spanning the Saranac, this bridge stands near the site of the 1814 structure; its planks were torn up by the Americans and used to construct a breast-work on the river's south bank. Among the fighters here were Aiken's Volunteers, consisting of local teenagers who took up arms against the British and also acted as scouts and intelligence gatherers for the American forces before the battle.

MOOERS' HOUSE

Also on Bridge Street, the 1803 house was headquarters for American commander Alexander Macomb during the 1814 battle. A plaque

Mooers' House, Bridge Street, Plattsburgh

states: "In this house lived Benjamin Mooers, a lieutenant in the war of the American Revolution and a major general in the war of 1812–14." A British cannonball, fired from across the Saranac, hit this house and it is still lodged in a wall. The house is in private ownership and is not open to the public.

RIVERSIDE CEMETERY

Between North Catherine Street and Steltzer Road, this old, tree-shaded burial ground contains the bodies of British and American officers killed in the land and water battles. They lie around the granite tomb of Capt. George Downie, commander of the British fleet, who was killed aboard the *Confiance*.

Tour to Valcour Island Battle Site

To view the scene of Benedict Arnold's famed battle, take the following short tour that begins at the Interpretive Center. Also along the way are two important sites pertaining to the War of 1812.

Directions
From the Interpretive Center, proceed south on US 9. Just over 2 miles, turn left at the sign for Clinton Community College and follow the winding drive to the large main campus building. Park in the visitor spaces and obtain a visitor pass at the ground-floor entrance.

OLD CHAMPLAIN HOTEL

The predecessor of this former resort hotel once served as William McKinley's summer White House and hosted presidents Theodore Roosevelt and Grover Cleveland. In the lobby is the anchor of Macdonough's ship, the *Preble*, and a plaque notes that it serves as a memorial to the historian Dennis Lewis, who died in 1997 and once taught history at Clinton Community College. Nearby is a British cannon captured by the French at Fort William Henry in 1757, just before the massacre. It was later placed aboard a French ship and was recovered from the bottom of Plattsburgh Bay. Walk from the lobby to the terrace that overlooks the bay and see the best of all views of the two naval battle sites. To the north is little Crab Island, southern anchor of the American battle line in 1814, with the monument to the American and British dead prominently in view. Beyond is Cumberland Head, which the British rounded in their 1814 attack. To the right are Valcour Island and the channel between island and mainland that Arnold defended in fateful 1776.

From the college, return to US 9 and continue south. In a little over 2 miles, turn left at the PERU DOCK sign on the left. This boat launch provides a fine view of the lighthouse on Valcour Island, and is located just north of the point where Arnold's little navy blocked the channel against the British advance from the south.

Return to US 9 and go south a little less than 1.5 miles. On the left, by the shore, see the monument commemorating the 1776 battle. Do not stop, but continue south noticing an old stone house on the right. The Gilliland House stood in 1814 and was witness to an event that might best be described as a "Dunkerque in reverse." Early on in World War II, British civilians crossed the English Channel in a huge fleet of privately owned boats to evacuate their soldiers from embattled Dunkerque, in France, under German attack. In 1814, scores of small private boats of all shapes and sizes brought volunteers from Vermont to battle the British invasion at Plattsburgh. By this house, they scrambled ashore and many were given firearms. Then they stepped off north to face a British army that may have been the best in the entire world.

Turn around as soon as possible and return to the monument on the right. Be careful, for there's scarcely room to pull off. Located opposite the southern tip of Valcour, the following words are carved into the stone: COMMEMORATING THE VALOR OF AMERICAN FORCES LED BY BENEDICT ARNOLD AT THE BATTLE OF VALCOUR OCTOBER 11, 1776.

This monument, at least, bears the name of the man who did turn traitor, but without whom the American Revolution might have been a British victory. It was along this shore that Arnold's battered fleet escaped, single file, in the night, past the British fleet. Return north on US 9 to the roundabout by the Interpretive Center.

Tour of the Land Battle

From the roundabout, go north on US 9 into downtown Plattsburgh. Stay on US 9 and on reaching the imposing Victorian Clinton County Courthouse go left onto Court Street. Take your first right onto Oak Street, which is NY 22. Go north 1 mile and cross I-87, where the road becomes NY 374. Quickly bear right onto NY 22 north, the old Beekmantown Road, and in 1.7 miles, topping a rise, notice a small monument on the left at Culver Hill. Here the Americans made a brief stand, facing thousands of British regulars advancing along the road ahead. There is no place to stop by the monument, so proceed 0.2 mile and turn left on West Hill Road. Drive to the rise of ground and turn around. From here, American cannon fired on the British along Beekmantown Road. The small American force in this area must have been awed by the sight of 4,000 redcoats moving against them. Return to NY 22 and continue north and at the Y, bear right on Ashley Road, and stop at the cemetery, where men who fought at Culver Hill are buried.

Culver Hill Monument on the old Beekmantown Road

Return to NY 22 and drive south back over Culver Hill again noting the monument. Back at the I-87 juncture, proceed through it and go nearly a mile to the intersection of Tom Miller Road. You are following the British advance and on the right, at the intersection, an old marker notes the site of the Miller House, occupied by the British in 1814. Turn left on Tom Miller Road, which becomes Boynton Avenue, and in 0.5 mile look for Halsey Court, a short street on your left. Pull in and see a monument on the left to the engagement fought at Halsey Corners. The Americans contested the British advance here before pulling back across the Saranac to their prepared defenses. Return to Boynton Avenue and after 0.3 mile pull into the Knights of Columbus parking lot on the left. Walk a few yards along the sidewalk and come to the large white brick house that was appropriated by British Gen. Thomas Brisbane as his headquarters.

Continue on Boynton Avenue for 0.75 mile and turn right on Cornelia Street, which is NY 3. Drive 3.3 miles along heavily developed NY 3, pass beneath I-87, and come to a Y where NY 22B branches left. Take NY 22B and in 1.5 miles reach an iron bridge crossing the Saranac. Cross the bridge, park nearby, and walk to the old marker by the bridge. It notes that in a skirmish here, two British soldiers and a horse were killed. Here New York militia stopped the British probe aimed at finding a place to turn the American left flank.

Return the way you came on NY 22B and NY 3 for 3 miles and take I-87 south. In 1.5 miles slow down on your approach to the Saranac River Bridge. Look to the right from the bridge, and you will see a waterfall. Below it is a stretch of flat rock marking the ford crossed by 4,000 British infantrymen on September 11, 1814, in their main attack aimed at battering the American flank. Proceed to the next exit, Exit 36, and go right on NY 22. Quickly move onto I-87 north. It was in the sandy pinewoods to your right that the Vermonters and New Yorkers stopped the British advance in a brisk fight before the British retreated. On recrossing the Saranac River Bridge, look to the right. The British proceeded down the near bank of the river as they advanced into battle. (The area of the battle is known as Pike's Cantonment, as American soldiers under Zebulon Pike, the discoverer of Pike's Peak, camped here the winter of 1812–13.) Eventually, Plattsburgh hopes to open a portion of this section of the battlefield to visitors. But at present it is nearly impossible to reach and much of the fighting area is within the fence of the old airbase, planned to become the Clinton County Airport.

Return north on I-87 to Exit 39. Go right on NY 314, then left, or north, on US 9. You are now on the old Shore Road in the area where the British came under fire from Macdonough's ships as they marched toward Plattsburgh. This completes your Plattsburgh tour.

Directions

Go north on US 9 for 15 miles and turn right onto NY 9B. Follow NY 9B almost 4 miles and turn right onto Point au Fer Road.

Note: Inquire at the Interpretive Center about tour boats to Crab Island and Valcour Island.

Chapter Seventeen

The Northern Lake

POINT AU FER

Advancing up the lake in the fall of 1776 with his British army and accompanying fleet, Sir Guy Carleton ordered a blockhouse built at Point au Fer. The point was to be garrisoned by the British

Point au Fer is private property, though its main roads are public.

until 1796. Well before the Revolution, Point au Fer had already experienced a significant encounter with history. Moving down the lake in May 1760, Robert Rogers and his Rangers put in here and were met by a larger French force. The rangers prevailed, after a difficult battle in the swamps, described by John Cuneo in his book *Robert Rogers of the Rangers*: "Rogers, forewarned, selected his terrain carefully, anchoring his right flank against a swamp. The French attacked his left as expected. Lieutenant Farrington with seventy men slipped around the bog along the lakeshore to hit the French from the rear. When he opened his attack, Rogers 'pushed them in front.' Only a heavy downpour which allowed the enemy to scatter, saved the French from annihilation."

Touring Point au Fer

On entering Point au Fer Road, one quickly comes onto a causeway that passes through the swamps in which Rogers did battle. Continue for a mile, then turn left at a fork onto Scales Road. At the end of a long straight stretch, the road reaches a right-hand turn and becomes Point au Fer Road. Directly ahead is an old house that stands on the site of the British blockhouse. Continue on Point au Fer Road, which is a long circular drive, and return to NY 9B.

Directions

Continue north on NY 9B and 1.5 miles along, the graceful Rouses Point Bridge comes in view. Pass through the village of Rouses Point and turn right onto US 2 leading to Vermont. Fort Montgomery is visible from the bridge, to the north, but the best view is from the parking lot at the Vermont end of the bridge on the left. The huge fort appears much smaller than from close up.

FORT MONTGOMERY

Soon after the War of 1812 the U.S. government, intent on preventing another British invasion along the lake, ordered construction of a fortification just south of the Canadian border, on Island Point. Work proceeded on the two-bastioned fort from 1816 to 1818. The next year a survey of the border revealed that the fort was on Canadian soil and the place gained the nom de guerre "Fort Blunder." All was held in abeyance until 1842 when, with the signing of the Webster-Ashburton Treaty, the border was moved a bit north and Island Point was finally, officially, made part of the United States. Two years later work began on a much larger fort, a five-bastioned stone edifice called Fort Montgomery. Thirty years in construction and designed by the famed builder of American forts, Joseph Totten, Fort Montgomery was planned to accommodate 800 men and 125 guns. As the Civil War came on, work was speeded up on the 3-plus-acre complex and just after the St. Albans Raid in 1864, the fort's guns were fired, perhaps a warning to those north of the border

The fort is on private property and because of vandalism, and the dangerous condition of the crumbling structure, visits are prohibited. Law enforcement patrols the site.

Fort Blunder, as seen from the Champlain Bridge at Rouses Point.

against future incursions. The fort was never garrisoned, though for many years it stood ready to be manned by troops from the nearby military base at Plattsburgh, should an emergency arise. Never fully completed, construction was suspended in 1870. Two years later, 57 guns were mounted, including 10 big 10-inch Rodman rifles that fired 124-pound shells. By 1886, the number of guns had been increased to 74. Sometime after the Civil War, the fort was visited by a major figure of that war, William Tecumseh Sherman, who believed the fort should be garrisoned full time, but it never happened. In 1937, in the Great Depression, with a nationwide need for jobs, the fort was partially dismantled with its stone used to build a bridge across Champlain at Rouses Point. Though much destroyed, as seen from the south and east, Fort Montgomery maintains a considerable look of invincibility.

Directions
After viewing Fort Blunder, return to US 2 and go east into Vermont for 4 miles, passing through Alburg. Turn right on West Shore Road, drive 4 miles and turn right onto VT 129, and cross the bridge to Isle La Motte. Follow signs to Saint Anne's Shrine. Just before entering the shrine, on the left, is a monument marking the 1775 encampment of

General Montgomery and 1,200 men moving to join the invasion of Canada. Drive downhill into the shrine, and park in the vicinity of the large outdoor church.

ISLE LA MOTTE

Champlain was the first European to see Isle La Motte when he moved up the lake in 1609. Champlain may well have camped here. Samuel Elliot Morison called Champlain "one of the greatest pioneers, and colonists of all time." Born in Brittany in 1570, Champlain made his first trip across the Atlantic after a stint in the French army spent fighting the Spanish. He sailed six times to the West Indies; then in 1603 he was invited to join a voyage to Canada. On arrival, he fell in love with the magnificent site of Québec on the St. Lawrence River. After an exploratory trip along the Maine coast, Champlain was back in France where he won permission from the King to establish a colony at Québec. In 1609, he joined Algonquin Indians in a retaliatory raid against the Iroquois who had been staging raids into Québec. On July 12, the party reached the Richelieu's rapids at Chambly and, 25 miles later, Champlain entered the great lake for the first time.

Saint Anne's Shrine, with masses conducted by the Edmundite Brothers, is open from mid-May through mid-October, though you're free to stop at any other time and walk about. You may wish to go first to the statue of Samuel de Champlain by the lake.

Indians were still harassing French colonists in 1666 when Pierre de St. Paul, Sieur de la Motte, was sent to build a fort on the Lake Champlain island that bears his name. Fort Saint Anne was the southernmost of five forts built as protection and as staging areas for French expeditions against the Indians. It likely had a double palisade 15 feet high and with a bastion in each corner.

The first Catholic Mass in Vermont was delivered here by Father Dubois, a regimental chaplain, probably out-of-doors, in the summer of 1666. When Bishop Laval, Canada's first Bishop, arrived in 1668, he found a proper chapel awaiting him, along with a small congrega-

Saint Anne's Shrine, Isle La Motte

tion, the first white settlement in Vermont. Why the fort was abandoned in 1671 is unknown; perhaps it was too distant to supply easily. Today the Edmundite Brothers maintain the Catholic Shrine of Saint Anne, where the French fort and settlement once stood.

Touring Saint Anne's Shrine

On entering the shrine area, you'll quickly see the large open-air church where Mass is celebrated. Across the road are the Stations of the Cross, in the area where the French fort stood. Indeed, it is believed that the piles of rock that support each station are from the fort's foundation. The stations may well outline the long disappeared little fort. Walk within this shaded area and you'll walk where the first white settlers of Vermont once lived. On summer days when services are taking place across the road, the incantations of the first Christian religion that white men brought to this part of the New World can be heard: "Hail Mary full of grace . . . "

Just north of the fort site is the large statue of Champlain, looking up his lake with an Indian companion. Across the street, adjacent to the church, Saint Anne's Shrine maintains a small history room. Walk south along the road from the open-air church and look to the hillside on the left. There stands the impressive golden statue of Our Lady of Lourdes. The statue, which once stood atop the tower of the Catholic cathedral in Burlington, miraculously survived a 1972 fire that destroyed the grand stone sanctuary.

Directions

Retrace your route 12 miles to Rouses Point and, on reaching the New York end of the bridge, turn north on US 11 and quickly come to the international boundary and Canadian customs. US 11 becomes CAN 223 in Canada; follow it 4 miles to a sign indicating a left turn to the Lacolle Blockhouse, which is visible from the road. Park in the lot just past the little fort.

LACOLLE BLOCKHOUSE

Lacolle's small rough-hewn blockhouse in the midst of Québec's pleasant farmland stands in stark contrast to the countryside's large white barns and neat houses. Square, made of logs, with an overhanging second story, and stone foundations, hundreds of such structures once

Lacolle Blockhouse

stood in North America. Of the 25 built in Canada, only Lacolle's remains. Constructed in 1781, in the Revolution's waning days, it was an important part of the British defense network, providing a military outpost near the border. At the time of its construction, the British still controlled Champlain's northern end, with Lacolle serving as a link between the British post at Point au Fer and fortified Île-aux-Noix, farther north on the Richelieu. The blockhouse stands on the banks of the Lacolle River, built to protect an important sawmill that once stood there.

> The blockhouse is open daily, mid-June through mid-September, 9:30–5:30; the blockhouse is open only weekends, mid-May through mid-June and from September 1 through mid-October. Free admission.

During the War of 1812, a battle occurred at Lacolle on the misty day of March 30, 1814, when British troops held the blockhouse and the nearby stone mill against an invading American force of 4,000 men. It was a hard-luck day for the attackers. The American commander divided his force and, advancing through the fog, the two columns fired upon each other. Also, the wet ground prevented the arrival of American artillery. Finally, the Americans did turn their muskets on the enemy. But after several hours of combat, they were forced to withdraw when British reinforcements arrived from Île-aux-Noix.

Touring the blockhouse

The building is original and contains exhibits on its history. You can still see loopholes in the log walls through which muskets were fired. Upstairs are embrasures where six cannon were posted. The best is outside, on the south wall, where the marks left by bullets and cannonballs from the 1814 clash are visible. Also, note the remains of a tunnel that once led from the blockhouse to the riverbank through which soldiers could escape.

Directions

From the blockhouse, return to CAN 223 and continue north. Six miles along, upon entering the village of St. Paul, turn right at the large sign marking the entrance to Fort Lennox and proceed to the banks of the Richelieu River and the fort's parking lot and Visitors Center. Before you, in the middle of the Richelieu, is Île-aux-Noix.

Chapter Eighteen

The Richelieu River Forts

ÎLE-AUX-NOIX AND FORT LENNOX

Samuel de Champlain wrote in his 1609 journal that he came on an island covered with nut trees. Île-aux-Noix, the "Isle of Nuts," got its name in the mid-1700s when a retired French captain who had served at Fort St. Frederic was allowed to reside on the island for the rental fee of a bag of nuts every year. At the time, the island was covered with nut-bearing trees. The once quiet little island was destined to play a part in three wars, beginning when the first of three forts was built there in 1759.

Purchase tickets in the Visitors Center by the parking lot. Fort Lennox is open daily, mid-May through late June, 10–5, June through September, 10–6, September through mid-October on weekends, 10–6. The short boat ride to the fort is included in the ticket. Admission fee.

As General Amherst prepared to make his powerful advance down the corridor in 1759, the French strategy was to delay the enemy as long as possible at Forts Carillon and St. Frederic, then make a last stand at Île-aux-Noix. The hope in Québec was that, in Europe, a peace could be signed before France lost Canada. That summer,

Note: On entering Canada from the United States, note that distances, and speed limits, are now given in kilometers, each equaling about 0.6 mile. Or, coming from the north, on crossing the border, remember that mileage is now just that, mileage.

Chevalier de Bourlemarque fortified the island constructing breast-works for 3,000 men and three batteries, on the island's southern end and on each side to prevent the passage of ships. Palisades were raised in place, ditches dug, and earthen walls piled up.

Not until August 16, 1760, did the siege of Île-aux-Noix begin, as 3,400 British landed on the Richelieu's eastern shore and built a mile-long breastwork to protect four batteries. Behind the fort's walls waited its new commander, Louis-Antoine de Bougainville, with 1,400 poorly equipped and supplied men. After 11 days of pounding, Bougainville evacuated the island in the night, his men quietly rowing to the Richelieu's western shore and slipping away through enemy lines. When the British entered the quiet fort next morning, they found just 30 privates and a good many sick and wounded soldiers. Montréal surrendered on September 8, surrounded by 18,000 troops, ending French rule in Canada. The last battle of New France had been fought at Île-aux-Noix. Amherst visited the island in October and or-dered its fortifications destroyed, carrying off anything salvageable for his new fort at Crown Point.

With war having returned to the Champlain Corridor in 1775, Congress ordered Philip Schuyler to invade Canada. General Richard Montgomery landed at Île-aux-Noix on September 4, using the place as a staging area for the invasion. But at the siege of Québec, Montgomery was killed and his broken and dispirited army retreated to Île-aux-Noix. Eventually, 7,000 American soldiers were camped on the crowded isle, many victims of smallpox. Schuyler hurried boats to the island to evac-uate the men to Crown Point. Many remained behind in lonely graves.

Sir Guy Carleton then occupied the island before his unsuccessful move south up Champlain. The next year, 1777, Burgoyne started from Île-aux-Noix with his grand army bound for defeat at Saratoga. The British kept the island as a base for harassing raids against the Americans. As the war ended, the British maintained a small garrison and Île-aux-Noix became a haven for Loyalist Americans forced to leave their homes south of the border.

The War of 1812 saw the island in use once again by the British, this time as a shipyard and base for their inland navy. Many of the

British ships that fought at Plattsburgh were built here. After the war, with the Americans building Fort Montgomery on the border, from 1819 to 1829 the British built a major fortification at Île-aux-Noix. And they built the place of American stone, quarried on Isle La Motte. Fort Lennox, named for a governor general of Canada, Charles Lennox, served as a border post. The place was garrisoned by Royal Canadian Rifles from 1840 until 1870. Nearly three-quarters of a century later Île-aux-Noix was again touched by war as Fort Lennox became a camp for Jewish refugees from Hitler's Europe.

Touring Île-aux-Noix

Fort Lennox is the best preserved of all the forts along the Champlain Corridor. After a short walk from the boat dock, one crosses a bridge over the moat, in which lily pads and frogs abound, and passes through a large stone gateway emerging onto a vast green lawn, the parade ground. The place today has the look of a well-kept college campus, with its stately stone buildings designed in the style of the British Regency. High green ramparts surround the place, giving it a sense of cool and restrained beauty, much in contrast to the disease, hunger, despair, and suffering that once prevailed among the American army retreating from Canada.

Take time to tour the fort's buildings, one of which contains a detailed model of Fort Lennox under construction. The old barracks are maintained as they would have appeared when garrisoned by soldiers early in the fort's life. Bunks are carefully made to regulations, and weapons and equipment hang in perfect order, at the ready, over the beds. Footlockers are stenciled with the names of men of the 24th regiment, which served at Lennox. Walk about the parade ground and cross the moat to the outer defenses of a 19th-century fortification in an almost perfect state of preservation. But do not look for a cemetery. Though hundreds of men, many of them American, are buried somewhere on the island, Parks Canada, which operates the fort, does not search for graves. So soldiers rest undisturbed, and unmarked, in some of the most historic soil of the Champlain Corridor.

Directions

From the Fort Lennox parking lot, turn north of CAN 223 and drive 9-plus miles to a Y in the road and a modernistic sculpture. Bear right onto rue Jacques-Cartier and in 2.5 miles you'll see the brick buildings of a military post on your right. Turn right through the gate and stop at the gatehouse. You will be directed to the Fort St. Jean Museum, the small brick building with the peaked roof to the left.

FORT ST. JEAN

A fort was first built by the French circa 1666 at St. Jean as part of their defenses against Indian raids that included the little fortification at Isle La Motte. That fort had fallen into ruin when, in 1748, with concern building about British intentions along the corridor, the French set about constructing a larger fortification at St. Jean. Swedish naturalist Peter Kalm wrote: "The French in Canada call the gnats 'marangoins' . . . these insects are in such prodigious numbers in the woods around St. Jean, that it would more properly be called 'Fort des Marangoins.'" An important port city and shipyard developed around the fort.

The Fort St. Jean Museum is open June 23 through August 22, Wednesday through Sunday, 10–5.

As the American Revolution commenced, St. Jean was again in the midst of war. On May 18, 1775, after the capture of Ticonderoga, Arnold sailed north and attacked the fort at St. Jean and its skimpy garrison, capturing boats and supplies. On returning up the lake, Arnold met Ethan Allen coming north on his own mission to St. Jean. But upon arrival, when a large British force appeared, Allen withdrew to Crown Point. Those actions caused the British to strengthen the small fort with sod walls and stockades.

An American invasion force arrived on September 6, 1775. Three assaults on Fort St. Jean were repulsed by expert British cannoneers, so the Americans laid siege. Meanwhile, Ethan Allen moved north against Montréal, on the mission that resulted in his capture. At St. Jean, the garrison weakened and grew short of supplies as the Ameri-

Fort St. Jean Museum

cans continued shelling. During the siege, a force of 50 Americans and 300 Canadian supporters managed to float past the fort and capture Fort Chambly to the north. Sir Guy Carleton sent a relief expedition, but Seth Warner's Green Mountain Boys turned it back. The fort at St. Jean surrendered on November 2.

In American hands, St. Jean was used as an important supply base. With the American failure at Québec, Benedict Arnold briefly withdrew his troops here, but soon Carleton marched in. At St. Jean, he reassembled the fleet that had been taken apart at Chambly and moved in pieces past the formidable rapids of the Richelieu. After Carleton's failed move up Champlain, Burgoyne was at St. Jean eight months later, gathering his army.

Though St. Jean's shipyards were used by the British during the War of 1812, the fort saw no action. In 1867, the place became a Canadian army base and many of Canada's famous regiments were stationed here before crossing the Atlantic to fight in two world wars. In 1952, it became the Saint Jean Royal Military College, training future officers for the Canadian forces. No longer a military operation, the place houses a preparatory school.

Visiting Fort St. Jean

Go first to the small museum, built in 1850 and once the post guard-house, where the history of Fort St. Jean is told through exhibits. Artifacts on display range from prehistoric times, through the American siege of the fort, to trophies brought from Europe during the world wars by Canadian regiments. Then walk about the old military post.

Cannon at Fort St. Jean on the Richelieu River

You will find that long banks of earth wind among the buildings, the old ramparts of the British fort. It is hard to imagine that here in this quiet riverside place, American soldiers once rained shot and shell into a surrounded British garrison.

Directions
From Fort St. Jean, turn right and bear right at the Y that you soon reach. For the next 12 miles, some of which pass through the busy streets of the city of St. Jean, follow the bank of the Richelieu closely as possible. The drive is an interesting one, along the river and the canal beside it, passing several locks, and once crossing the canal on a narrow bridge. In 12 miles you'll see a pleasant shaded park on the right. Turn in and park at Fort Chambly.

FORT CHAMBLY

The first view of Fort Chambly may well be the most surprising you'll encounter at any historic site in the corridor. The stone fort, its high stone walls pierced by narrow slits, is startling; one simply does not expect to see what resembles a medieval keep on a North American river. But here it is in the midst of a busy Canadian city on the very edge of the Richelieu where its mighty rapids end. Here the great river curves and one sees the spires of distinctly French churches along the far bank and the rise of distant mountains. The interpretive signs at the fort repeat the phrase, "The rapids remember," and indeed, there is much history at Fort Chambly. A sign near the entrance says, THE RAPIDS REMEMBER WHEN THE AMERINDIANS ESTABLISHED ENCAMPMENTS ON THE BANKS OF THE RICHELIEU WELL BEFORE THE EUROPEANS SAILED THESE WATERS FOR THE FIRST TIME IN 1609.

Chambly is woven into the history of New France, beginning when Champlain encountered the long rapids in 1609, having expected to row unimpeded south to the "Great Lake of the Iroquois." In July 1665, Capt. Jacques de Chambly of the Carignan-Salières

Open daily, March through November, 9–5. Admission fee.

Fort Chambly

Regiment arrived to build a fort by the rapids, a simple wooden square made of cedar and named for a Catholic saint, St. Louis. Over the years, the fort fell toward ruin and in 1693 the place was rebuilt. But Fort St. Louis burned in 1702 when a chaplain accidentally set himself and the fort afire. Again, the fort was rebuilt. When the raiding party that sacked Deerfield, Massachusetts, in 1704 reached Chambly, the minister John Williams wrote that the garrison treated him and fellow captives with kindness.

With the English looking toward Canada to retaliate against such raids as the bloody Deerfield event, in 1709 the French began building a stone fort at Chambly that they hoped would be capable of withstanding artillery fire. The work was supervised by Josue Dubois Berthelot de Beaucours, New France's chief engineer. The fort eventually lost strategic importance with the completion of Fort St. Frederic at Crown Point, and its guns were moved south to that new bastion.

With Amherst's invasion of Canada, Chambly surrendered to the British on September 1, 1760. But 15 years later, the British were on the defensive when, in the fall of 1775, the Americans invaded Canada. During the siege of St. Jean, an American force under Maj.

John Brown and James Livingston forced Chambly to surrender. By late spring, the Americans were in retreat, stopping only briefly at Chambly with the British in hot pursuit of the disease-ridden army. American Gen. John Thomas and other American soldiers died here and were buried in unmarked graves near the fort. As the Americans departed, they set fire to the place.

Additional buildings were added during the War of 1812, and the fort became headquarters for the 1814 campaign to Plattsburgh. In 1869, the British army gave up the fort and in the 1870s it began to collapse into a picturesque ruin. Fortunately, a journalist, Joseph Octave Dion, a Chambly native, refused to let this monument to New France disappear. He moved into the fort and, from 1886 until his death in 1916, worked on its restoration.

Touring Fort Chambly

From the parking lot, walk north through the lovely riverside park to the fort's entrance. Above the portal in the fort's grand façade are the arms of the king of France with their massive lilies. Passing through the gateway, the visitor enters a courtyard typical of French 18th-century domestic architecture, a decided contrast to the grim outer walls. Now restored to its 1750 appearance, the fort is a museum depicting the life of colonists of 18th-century Canada and of soldiers who garrisoned it 250 years ago.

Fittingly, the northernmost of our sites contains a large and modernistic relief map of the Champlain Corridor, which helps put the geography of the area, and its key historic sites, in perspective. A video depicts not only the fort's long history, but also its preservation. Be sure to climb to the top floor in the fort's northwest corner, where narrow stairs lead up into one of the fort's tiny lookout posts. You'll see the Richelieu as a French soldier of long ago looked for the approach of an enemy. On leaving the fort, walk north to the cemetery area. Buried there, principally in unmarked graves, are many of the British, French, American, and Canadian soldiers who died at Fort Chambly. A monument notes that among them is General Thomas, who perished on June 2, 1776, on the smallpox-riddled retreat from Canada.

Directions

Turn left on leaving the Chambly parking lot going south along the river the way you came, following CAN 223. In 9 miles on entering the city of St. Jean, be sure to watch for signs that keep you on CAN 223, which moves away from the river. In 2-plus miles, after going through an underpass, turn right onto CAN 219 South, looking carefully for the route sign. Proceed some 12 miles through the fertile farming country of southern Québec and on entering the village of Napierville, turn right on CAN 221 at a small, triangular green. Follow signs for AUT 15 and in 2.5 miles turn right on AUT 15 South. Route 15 becomes I-87 at the international border. Follow I-87 south just under 40 miles to Exit 34, and take NY 9N south. Go about 16 miles into the village of Jay and turn right on NY 86. Along the way, the lovely Au Sable River winds and splashes by the roadside. All the while the mountains become higher until you round a curve and confront a great upland valley dominated by 4,800-foot Whiteface Mountain. In 16 miles, after passing along the base of towering Whiteface, on entering the village of Lake Placid, famed for hosting two Winter Olympics, turn left on NY 73. In 2 miles you'll come to a sign for the John Brown Farm; turn right into its long driveway. The towers of the two huge Olympic ski jumps, sadly, loom above the historic place.

Chapter Nineteen

The John Brown Farm

A CASE CAN BE MADE that the Civil War became inevitable the day John Brown rode from his farm in the Adirondacks, bound away to raid the arsenal and armory at Harpers Ferry and, hopefully, to start a slave uprising. From the time Brown struck that quiet village, where the Shenandoah River flows into the Potomac, the nation seems to have been set on an unswerving course to war. Brown came home in a pine box, his famous body destined to "moulder away" in a grave in his own front yard. Events moved fast after his little uprising, capture, and hanging. In not more than two years vast northern armies went tramping down the roadways of the American South, singing the marching song "John Brown's Body" that proclaimed the old man's soul, too, "goes marching on." And soon Julia Ward Howe set to its music the words,

> Mine eyes have seen the glory of the coming of the Lord.
>
> He is tramping out the vintage where the grapes of wrath are stored.

The fateful lightning had been loosed upon the land, and this "Battle Hymn of the Republic" would resound until the secessionist states were subdued and the slaves, in law at least, had been set free.

Brown came to North Elba in 1849 to live among free blacks given land by the wealthy abolitionist Gerrit Smith, in a North Elba

The John Brown Farm, North Elba, New York

community called "Timbucto." Brown, it is said, had been an avowed enemy of slavery since his boyhood when he saw a young black friend beaten. In North Elba, near Whiteface Mountain, Brown farmed and, with his second wife, Mary Ann Day, raised a large family. Then he set off for Kansas to join his homesteading sons in a land being disputed by anti-slavery and pro-slavery forces. The Browns quickly pitched into the fighting, winning a victory at Osawatomie, also hacking to death five settlers they believed to be supporters of slavery. Thereafter, Brown was back at North Elba only intermittently, sometimes going down and across the lake to Vergennes for provisions.

In 1859, he was bound for Harpers Ferry, on a course that would make him, in the North, a martyr to the cause of freedom, but in the South, an anathema. On the night of October 16, 1859, Brown and his followers assaulted the Harpers Ferry armory and arsenal, planning to use its weapons to arm liberated slaves. Captured on October 18, Brown was imprisoned at Charles Town, Virginia, tried by the Commonwealth of Virginia, and hanged on December 2, 1859. Shortly before his execution, Brown prophesied: "I, John Brown, am quite certain that the crimes of this guilty land will never be purged away but with blood." Mary Ann Brown journeyed to Virginia to visit her doomed husband, then brought his body back home, by train to Vergennes, by ferry to the New York shore, then by wagon up the steep and winding mountain roads to North Elba. It was John Brown's wish that he be buried on his farm, and six days after his execution his body was lowered to the cold earth beside a large boulder in the front yard. The funeral was held in the small parlor of the Brown farmhouse, a service that began with the singing of Brown's favorite hymn, "Blow Ye the Trumpet, Blow!" A large crowd of friends, admirers, and the curious watched outside and strained to hear as Brown's fellow abolitionist Wendell Phillips delivered a eulogy. Reverend Joshua Young said the final words, at the grave: "I have fought a good fight, I have finished my course, I have kept the faith."

Mary Ann Brown stayed on the farm until 1863, when she moved the family to California. In 1895, the Brown place at North Elba, including all 244 acres the Browns owned, was given to New York State to become an historic site.

Touring the Brown Farm

Begin at the farmhouse. The house is almost all original, including floorboards walked by the Browns. The parlor, where the funeral was held, contains several pieces of furniture that belonged to the Browns, including their table and chairs. Brown, a family man who loved to sit by the fire, spent much time in this room. During the open-casket funeral service, the abolitionist Philips preached here for two hours. Upstairs, you can see the signature of one of the black settlers of Timbucto, Lyman Eps, written on a ceiling board, apparently at the time the house was built.

Open May through October, Wednesday through Saturday, 10–5, and Sunday, 1–5; also open Memorial Day, Independence Day, and Labor Day. Admission fee.

At the end of the funeral, Brown's open casket was placed on the flat rock by the front door, in order to give the crowd that had waited outside a last look. Then the casket was closed and taken beside the large glacial boulder, beside which Brown had told his wife he wished

Parlor, John Brown House

to be buried. Brown had often enjoyed sitting by the boulder, especially at evening. Note that Brown's name is carved in the great rock, done in 1866 at the insistence of Col. Francis Lee, a Civil War hero, afraid that souvenir hunters might destroy the small gravestone. Today, the grave and boulder are enclosed by an iron fence; the Brown gravestone is protected by glass. Brown lay by himself until 1883 when other victims of the Harpers Ferry Raid began to be moved to North Elba. Now 10 raiders lie beside their captain.

The barn, south of the house, offers an exhibit and video. Within the farm's circular driveway is a statue of Brown, walking with a black child, arm on his shoulder, guiding him north. The statue faces north, toward freedom.

Directions
From the Brown Farm, return to NY 73 and turn right, east, traveling the winding road down through the communities of Keene, Keene Valley, and St. Huberts, with grand mountains rising everywhere. In 26 miles ease onto NY 95, and in 2 miles take I-87 south to the second exit. There take NY 74 east 18 miles and on the outskirts of Ticonderoga, turn onto NY 9N south. In 1.5 miles, on coming alongside the Ticonderoga Golf Club, look for a marker near the site of Rogers Rangers' famous 1758 "Battle of the Snowshoes." Continuing south, look for an historic marker by a vegetable stand on the left. It states that Rogers retreated through the pass ahead, following an old Indian trail, after the battle. A little more than 1.5 miles south, on the left side, is the entrance to the Rogers Rock State Campground. From near the campground, Rogers Rock rises on the shore of Lake George.

Chapter Twenty

Rogers Country

ROGERS ROCK

This steep, rocky hill dominates the northern end of 32-mile-long Lake George. Locals say that the French maintained a lookout post atop it most of the time they occupied Ticonderoga. Legend has it that Rogers escaped French and Indian pursuers by feigning having leaped to his death down the rock's sheer face. It is said he threw his belongings down and then fled on snowshoes worn backwards to disguise his direction. Campground workers discourage inquiries about climbing Rogers Rock, noting that to reach it, private property must be crossed. Also, from experience, the climb is difficult, even dangerous. As you drive south on NY 9N, look for glimpses of the precipitous hill behind you and to the left. But the best way to see Rogers Rock is from a Lake George tour boat.

Directions
From Rogers Rock Campground, continue south on US 9 North as it skirts the lakeshore, with views toward the unspoiled east shore. Some 9 miles south, the highway passes through the village of Sabbathday Point, and a mile beyond stop at a turnoff on the left with a fine view of the northern lake. A marker gives a brief history of Lake George.

Just north of here, near Sabbathday Point which protrudes into the lake from the near shore, Indians ambushed an English scouting party from Fort William Henry traveling by boat on July 26, 1757, killing 160 men. From the parking area, the road turns from the lake and ascends into the wilds behind Tongue Mountain. The next 8 miles pass through mountainous woodlands—Rogers Country.

ROGERS COUNTRY

Robert Rogers of New Hampshire led a band of men through the wilds around Lake George and Lake Champlain, doing battle time and again with the hated French, winning for himself and his wily band a place in history, and legend. Books and stories have been written of Rogers' Rangers, and a film based on the Kenneth Roberts novel *Northwest Passage*, in which Rogers was played by Spencer Tracy, portrayed their raid on the St. Francis Indian village. When Rogers came from beyond the Connecticut River to offer his services to the English in 1756, he was already familiar with the no-man's-land that lay between the English forts Edward and William Henry and the French bastions of Carillon (at Ticonderoga) and Crown Point. This was a thickly forested, mountainous land of sudden deep valleys where men lay in ambush, where war parties moved silently, where English, French, and Indians were ever in danger of sudden death, capture, scalping. Rogers, often based on Rogers Island at Fort Edward, time and again ventured north to the vicinity of the French forts, ambushing patrols and sentries, bringing prisoners to the English for interrogation. He spied on the French forts from nearby heights or moved in the night to their walls. Rogers and his men were active at all seasons of the year, prowling forth on snowshoes or, sometimes, on skates on the long lakes. His men knew the ways of the wilds, existing for days in subzero weather, living off the frozen landscape. They became men of the land.

This next-to-the-last leg of our long journey—through the upper Hudson, Lake George, Lake Champlain, and the Richelieu Corridor—provides a wonderful reminder that this vast landscape once was, in-

Rogers' Rangers as observed by Francis Parkman

"These rangers wore a sort of woodland uniform, which varied in the different companies, and were armed with smooth-bore guns, loaded with buckshot, bullets, or sometimes both. The best of them were commonly employed on Lake George; and nothing can surpass the adventurous hardihood of their lives. Summer and winter, day and night, were alike to them. Embarked in whaleboats or birch-canoes, they glided under the silent moon or in the languid glare of the breathless August day, when islands floated in dreamy haze, and the hot air was thick with odors of the pine; or in the bright October, when the jay screamed from the woods, squirrels gathered their winter hoard, and congregated blackbirds chattered farewell to their summer haunts; when gay mountains basked in light, maples dropped leaves of rustling gold, sumachs glowed like rubies under the dark green of the unchanging spruce, and mossed rocks with all their painted plumage lay double in the watery mirror; that festal evening of the year, when jocund Nature disrobes herself, to wake again refreshed in the joy of her undying spring. Or, in the tomb-like silence of the winter forest, with breath frozen on his beard, the ranger strode on snow-shoes over the spotless drifts; and, like Durer's knight, a ghastly death stalked ever at his side. There were those among them for whom this stern life had a fascination that made all other existence tame."

deed, wilderness. It is a land of beaver meadows, swift streams, cascades, tall pines and ledges, with signs that warn against disturbing the rattlesnakes. The mountains are steep and the forests deep. This was the domain of Native Americans, then of the Rangers, moving often behind the mountains on the west shore of Lake George to spy on the French forts to the north. As you drive, look for parking areas where trails lead into the forest. Park in any and walk a way into the woods. Do you feel the history here from a time when danger stalked this landscape? Once this was primeval forest where men of another time made war.

Directions

Some 3 miles after NY 9N returns to the lakeshore, just north of the village of Bolton Landing, a sign points the way to I-87. Here turn right and in about 5 miles, on reaching I-87, turn south and drive 32 miles and take Exit 16. Turn west on Ballard Road, follow signs to Grant's Cottage, and after 2 miles turn right onto Mountain Road. The cottage is on the grounds of the Mount McGregor Corrections Facility, a New York state prison. Guards stop all cars and, quite sensibly, warn against picking up hitchhikers. It's 2 miles uphill from the Ballard Road turn to the right fork, among the prison buildings, that leads to the Grant Cottage.

Chapter Twenty-One

Grant's Cottage

THE COTTAGE

Ulysses S. Grant, who, with the possible exception of Abraham Lincoln, was the man most responsible for Union victory in the Civil War, died here on a summer morning in 1885. The victor of Forts Henry and Donelson, of Vicksburg, Petersburg, and, finally, Appomattox Court House, came to this cottage on Mount McGregor June 16, 1885, after having been diagnosed with an inoperable cancer of the throat. Nearly penniless after a series of poor investments, Grant had been approached the previous fall by Mark Twain about writing his wartime reminiscences, which Twain would publish. Grant accepted Twain's generous terms and, struggling as his condition worsened, he completed the manuscript at Mount McGregor just days before he died. The book was a huge success and Grant's family was left with a considerable fortune and the nation with one of its best, if not the best, eyewitness accounts of the Civil War.

The cottage is open Memorial Day to Labor Day, Wednesday through Sunday, 10–4; Labor Day to Columbus Day, Saturday and Sunday, 10–4.

At the time of the cancer diagnosis, Grant was living in New York City, but at the urging of his personal physician, he accepted an invitation to take up residence in a mountain cottage at the southern edge of the Adirondacks. It was felt that the cooler, dryer air would ease his suffering and prolong life. At the time, a railway spur led from Saratoga to a hotel on the summit of 1,040-foot Mount McGregor and Grant arrived at the cottage, just below the hotel, in mid-June. Though the cancer was already advanced and he could speak only with difficulty, Grant immediately set to work on his memoirs. As the disease progressed, the former president slept late to gain strength, then resumed work about noon, often writing in his determined hand until far into the night. Often, he worked on the cottage porch, dictating when his voice allowed.

As weeks passed, Grant steadily weakened, and a host of reporters gathered nearby to chronicle his final days. Visitors arrived by the hundreds, some in official delegations, but many curious and admiring people come for a last look at an American icon. One former Union soldier pitched his tent behind the cottage and acted as Grant's guard, keeping all at a respectful distance. In the evening, Grant continued writing in his sickroom at the rear of the cottage, seated in a pair of stuffed chairs pushed together to form a makeshift bed. He also slept there, for to lie down gave him a choking sensation.

On July 20, with the manuscript completed, Grant asked to be taken to an overlook on the mountainside, 400 yards from the cottage. Wheeled there in a wicker wheelchair-like contraption called a "bath wagon," Grant took in the long views across the Hudson Valley only until the men pulling and pushing his conveyance were rested for the uphill return trip. Back at the cottage, the general was exhausted, the modest excursion having taken a considerable toll on his strength. He expired at 8 AM on July 23, and upon his death his doctor stepped onto the porch and wiped his brow, a signal to the reporters that Grant was gone.

Touring the Cottage

The building has been preserved as it was at the moment when Grant died and most of the furnishings in the three downstairs rooms that are open to the public were present at that time. In the sickroom are the two chairs in which he slept. A pair of penciled notes are displayed that he wrote as death neared, one reading in part, "I am doing as well as can be expected and have held out longer." A tall bottle still contains the mixture of water and cocaine prescribed, along with injections of morphine and brandy, for pain. On a table in the large front room, where Grant greeted visitors, are two trays hammered out of Civil War lead bullets, in which calling cards were placed. Among them are those of Mark Twain and Simon Bolivar Buckner, a friend of Grant's from West Point days. Buckner, as a Confederate general, had capitulated to Grant at Fort Donelson on Grant's terms of unconditional surrender, terms that so angered Buckner the two had not spoken in more than 20 years. At the cottage, the old warriors had an amicable conversation, Buckner talking and Grant replying with handwritten notes. Both men wept.

On pleasant days, Grant sat on the cottage porch, in the wicker chair in the corner. The bed he died in is still covered by the bedspread under which he expired. Above the bed is a portrait of Lincoln, Grant's former commander in chief. Some said that as Grant breathed his last, sunlight illuminated the portrait, and, indeed, it faces a large eastern window. Beside it is a picture of Grant in military uniform. The clock on the mantel stands at 8:08, the time of death, stopped by his son Fred that morning at the moment. At 11 the previous night, Grant roused from seeming unconsciousness to note that the clock had struck 12 times at 11. "Fred," he whispered, "hadn't you better take that clock down and wind it up and start it as it should go?" Fourteen days before, Grant had written a note to his beloved wife, Julia: "I bid you farewell until we meet in another, and, I trust, better world. You will find this on my person after my demise."

The parlor dining-room table, where Grant took meals with his family when able, is also the table upon which his body was embalmed. A funeral service was held at the cottage and a now brittle floral tribute, sent by former soldiers, with a three-star emblem, is preserved. Grant's body was taken to New York City for a grand funeral that Julia was too bereaved to attend. Not until 1892 did she return to the cottage, signing the guest book, which is still displayed. From the cottage a path leads down to the eastern overlook visited by Grant four days before his death. A monument surrounded by an iron fence bears the words, THIS STONE MARKS THE SPOT WHERE GENERAL U. S. GRANT HAD HIS LAST VIEW OF THE VALLEY. The view is spectacular, across the broad Hudson Valley to the summits of the Taconic, Berkshire, and Green mountains. Some say Grant wanted to look again at a great battlefield, toward the historic fields of Saratoga.

Directions

Return to I-87 the way you came and proceed north or south, as your journey takes you. Your tour of the Champlain Corridor's military sites has come to an end. From this once bloodied landscape, go in peace.

Sources

Allen, Robert Willis. *Marching On!: John Brown's Ghost, from the Civil War to Civil Rights.* Northfield, Vt.: Northfield News and Printery, 2000.

Anderson, Fred. *Crucible of War: The Seven Years' War and the Fate of Empire in British North America, 1754–1766.* New York: Vintage Books, 2000.

Ansley, Norman. *Vergennes, Vermont, and the War of 1812.* Severna Park, Md.: Brooke Keefer Limited Editions, 1999.

Baldwin, Jeduthan. *Revolutionary Journal.* Bangor, Me.: The De-Burians, 1906.

Bellico, Russell P. *Chronicles of Lake Champlain: Journeys in War and Peace.* Fleischmanns, N.Y.: Purple Mountain Press, 1999.

———.*Sail and Steam in the Mountains: A Maritime and Military History of Lake George and Lake Champlain.* Fleischmanns, N.Y.: Purple Mountain Press Ltd., 2001.

Bradfield, Gerald E. *Fort William Henry: Digging Up History.* Lake George: The French and Indian War Society, 2001.

Bratten, John R. *The Gunboat* Philadelphia *and the Battle of Lake Champlain.* College Station: Texas A&M University Press, 2002.

Bulletin of the Fort Ticonderoga Museum XIV, no. 4 (Fall 1983), and XV, no. 1 (Winter 1988).

Burdick, Virginia Mason. *Captain Thomas Macdonough: Delaware-Born Hero of the Battle of Lake Champlain*. Wilmington, Del: Delaware Heritage Press, 1991.

Burgoyne, John. *A State of the Expedition from Canada as Laid Before the House of Commons by Lieutenant-General Burgoyne*. London: J. Almon, 1780.

———.*Orderly Book of Lieut. Gen. John Burgoyne*. Albany, N.Y: J. Munsell, 1860.

Calloway, Colin G. *The Western Abenakis of Vermont*. Norman: University of Oklahoma Press, 1990.

Charbonneau, André. *The Fortifications of Île aux Noix: A Portrait of the Defensive Strategy on the Upper Richelieu Border in the 18th and 19th Centuries*. Ottawa: Parks Canada, 1994.

Cohn, Arthur. *The Great Bridge. Report for the Lake Champlain Management Conference*. 1993.

Crockett, Walter Hill. *A History of Lake Champlain: The Record of Three Centuries, 1609–1909*. Burlington, Vt.: Hobart and Shanley & Company, 1909.

Cuneo, John. *Robert Rogers and His Rangers*. Ticonderoga, N.Y.: Fort Ticonderoga Museum, 1988.

Everest, Allan Seymour. *The War of 1812 in the Champlain Valley*. Syracuse, N.Y.: Syracuse University Press, 1981.

Fitz-Enz, Colonel David. *The Final Invasion: Plattsburgh, The War of 1812's Most Decisive Battle*. New York: Cooper Square Press, 2001.

Godwin, R. Christopher and Associates, Inc. *The Mount Independence State Historic Site Cultural Resource Management Plan*. Report for the Vermont Division of Historic Preservation, 1997.

Haviland, William A., and Marjory W. Power. *The Original Vermonters: Native Inhabitants Past and Present*. Hanover and London: University Press of New England, 1994.

Hill, Ralph Nading. *Lake Champlain Key to Liberty*. Taftsville, Vt.: The Countryman Press, 1977.

Historical Markers on the Crown Point Road: A Driver's Guide. Proctor, Vt.: Crown Point Road Association, 2004 edition.

Holbrook, Stewart H. *Ethan Allen.* New York: The Macmillan Co., 1940.

Jennings, Francis. *The Ambiguous Iroquois Empire.* New York: W.W. Norton & Company, 1984.

Kerlidou, Joseph J. *St. Anne of Isle La Motte.* Burlington, Vt.: The Free Press Association, 1895.

Ketchum, Richard. *Saratoga: Turning Point of America's Revolutionary War.* New York: Henry Holt and Co., 1997.

Lancaster, Bruce. *The American Revolution.* Boston: Houghton Mifflin Co., 1987.

Lord, Philip, Jr. *War Over Walloomscoick: Land Use and Settlement Pattern on the Bennington Battlefield–1777.* Albany: The University of the State of New York and the State Education Department, 1989.

Loring, Stephen. "Boundary Maintenance, Mortuary Ceremonialism and Resource Control in the Early Woodland: Three Cemetery Sites in Vermont." *Archaeology of Eastern North America* 13 (1985): 93–127.

Macdonough, Rodney. *Life of Commodore Thomas Macdonough, U.S. Navy.* Boston: The Fort Hill Press, 1909.

Martin, James Kirby. *Benedict Arnold, Revolutionary Hero: An American Warrior Reconsidered.* New York and London: New York University Press, 1997.

Millard, James P. *The Secrets of Crab Island.* South Hero, Vt.: America's Historic Lakes, 2002.

Parkman, Francis. *A Half-Century of Conflict.* New York: Collier Books, 1962.

Skaggs, David Curtis. *Thomas Macdonough, Master of Command in the Early U. S. Navy.* Annapolis: Naval Institute Press, 2003.

Starbuck, David R. *The Ferris Site on Arnold's Bay.* Basin Harbor, N.Y.: The Lake Champlain Maritime Museum, 1989.

————.*The Great Warpath: British Military Sites from Albany to Crown Point*. Hanover and London: University Press of New England, 1999.

————.*Massacre at Fort William Henry*. Hanover and London: University Press of New England, 2002.

————.*Rangers and Redcoats on the Hudson*. Hanover and London. University Press of New England, 2004.

Strach, Stephen G. *Some Sources for the Study of the Canadian Participation in the Military Campaign of Lieutenant-General John Burgoyne 1777*. Bulletin of the Eastern National Park and Monument Association, 1983.

————.*The Parkman Reader*. Boston and Toronto: Little, Brown & Company, 1955.

The Tour to the Northern Lakes of James Madison & Thomas Jefferson, May–June 1791. A facsimile edition, edited and with an introduction by J. Robert Maguire. Fort Ticonderoga, N.Y.: 1995.

Van de Water, Frederic F. *The Reluctant Republic: Vermont, 1724–1791*. New York: The John Day Company, 1941.

Index

Italic page numbers indicate illustrations.